Launch Out Into The Deep

"Let Your Nets Down for a Catch"
- Luke 5:4

By
Dr. Anita F. Mason

xulon
PRESS

Copyright © 2013 by Dr. Anita F. Mason

Launch Out Into The Deep
by Dr. Anita F. Mason

Printed in the United States of America

ISBN 9781625096029

Unless otherwise indicated, Bible quotations are taken from the New King James Version, (NKJV). Copyright © 1983 by Thomas Nelson, Inc.

Cover Design oil painting by: Anita Mason

www.xulonpress.com

This is a Time for Depth

A Time to Bless

A Time to Discern

A Time to Change your Environment

A Time to Envision your Future

A merry heart makes a cheerful countenance,
But by sorrow of the heart the spirit is broken.
Proverbs 15:13

Dedication

I dedicate this book to my family – Cliff my spouse, my sons Greg, Brian, and Todd, my daughter Meda Bateman, and all my grandchildren. A special dedication to our oldest son Dale and my sister Georgia Esker, who have gone before us to be with the Lord.

To my editors and readers, including my mentoring group (Tribe), thank you for helping me and encouraging me through the difficult times to push through to get this work finished.

And most of all, to my Lord and Savior. In Him "all things are possible."

Special Thanks

A special thanks to Julie Ebeling, Paula Wilson, and Susan Stukins for their editing and typing skills. Also, to Robyn Wells for her ongoing encouragement from beginning to end.

Contents

Foreword

From its captivating first pages, author, Dr. Anita Mason, takes us on a journey "Into the Deep" where it is obvious that the words written have not only been researched by the pricelessness of time and study, but by one called and dedicated to help set others free!

In my years of walking with this friend and mother of healing, I've been blessed to have Anita serve on the advisory board of PowerHouse Ministries, a ministry devoted to raising up a prophetic army for the end times harvest. The hours that Anita has spent before our followers have added depth and width to our tool belts – strengthening and enlightening all within the sound of her teaching.

Now, this energetic pioneer of the faith propels us forward to enter the corridor change, where yet another fresh spiritual state of consciousness is stirred as we read her book and glean insights for these trying days. Hidden places of fear, trauma, and areas related to the dark side of life, are automatically exposed as light is shed on *truths that set God's people free*. Places, where you didn't know how to respond to before, suddenly have a chance to be addressed with a new level and *power* of correct mental processing! With each page, one is reminded that God is greater.

In short, readers will be both delighted in the lighthearted nature of Dr. Mason's delivery, while enjoying the discovery of *information that brings transformation*!

Dr. Sandy Powell
PowerHouse Ministries, Inc.
Nashville, TN

I have known Anita Mason and have been her Pastor for over 30 years. Anita has served at Maranatha Assembly of God Church here in Decatur, Illinois in several capacities including being on staff as our Counseling Pastor. Anita has a great passion for teaching the Word of God and for mentoring others in their walk with the Lord.

Anita's ministry has been a great blessing to not only our church but also our entire community. What

Anita shares in her book comes from a lifetime of ministry experience. I know you will be blessed and helped as you read and apply Biblical truths you find here.

Pastor Doug Lowery
Pastor Maranatha Assembly of God Church
Decatur, Illinois

Dr. Anita Mason shows us how to take a thought and let God multiply it in substance. You will enjoy the journey through her field of gold nuggets. Many times the Lord speaks to each of us and we enjoy it, but do not write it down for the benefit of others. Thank you, Anita, for letting others in on your personal revelations and teachings that bless us all. There is much food for thought in her book and every big or little way we see the Lord and His Word in greater understanding, we are changed from the inside out.

Reverend Billie Landers
Next Generation Ministries, International
Auburn, IL

Since I have known Anita Mason, her focus, motivation, and passion has been to allow the Lord to use her to teach and lead Christians into a deeper understanding and more intimate knowledge of God, His Word, His spiritual principals, of prayer, of those things that enable us to walk in our full destinies.

For years, Anita has devoted her time to mentoring women, and eventually men, to develop their spiritual gifts and to function in agreement and union with our supernatural God. Anita's heart is to pass on those secret things the Lord reveals to her to those close to Him. And she relishes the privilege of passing it on to equip others as much as she delights in receiving it for herself. I have many times been a grateful recipient of a Holy Spirit impartation of knowledge and even anointing because of the ministry brought into my life by Anita. I have pages of notes from her teaching, the contents of which I've carried in my heart and applied in my life and passed on to others. On a very personal level, God used Anita through a prophetic Word to tell me that it was time to meet my husband, just shortly before God revealed my husband's identity to me.

So it is not surprising to me that God would have Anita continue to mentor and share His revelations in a book that can be highlighted, reread and passed on. I have no doubt that you will be blessed, taught and further equipped to be the person God created you to be through the reading of this book. That is God's heart, and it is Anita's to be used to advance His purposes in your life. Get ready to receive from Him as you read because He has much for you in these pages!

Mary Turek

Introduction

Go with me on my journey of life as we launch out into the deep. Every chapter will be different in subject matter. My principles, my thoughts and revelations with some of my innermost feelings and emotions about my spiritual journey are revealed in these pages.

I call many of my insights and revelations **Golden Nuggets of Truth** from the Lord. I seem to have some thought or opinion on everything I read and study. I'm not trying to be a "know it all", I just want to "know it all".

In this vein, I will carefully write about things or subjects that are truth for me and what I think are insightful revelations on God's Word.

One reminder I keep getting from the Holy Spirit is *"If I be lifted up I will draw all men unto me."* This is what this book is all about. Lifting Him up, resulting in growing deeper into His *mysteries* and *treasures* of life.

What Is Man?

God created man with a unique type of strength. He was to conquer all of the powers of darkness. Take the Promised Land and use his authority to build God's Kingdom on earth.

A man of God has a presence that no other man has. His voice booms through the atmosphere like arrows shot from a bow. His authority is a mountain that rises above every obstacle.

– Anita Mason 06/10/12

Launching Out

Unless you walk out into the unknown,
the odds of making a profound difference in your life are pretty low.

-Tom Peters (Bits & Pieces)

Launch out into the deep and let your nets down for a catch (Luke 5:4). This scripture has been a mystery for me for quite some time.

I first received this scripture from the Lord about ten years ago. I knew that there was a deep meaning from the Lord in this passage, but what was it? Since that time, I have been led to this scripture several more times. I asked myself what is deep to me and what is deep to you?

Writing this book has been like launching out into the deep. It is my belief that writing is one of the **stepping out into the deep** messages the Lord has urged me to do. My prayer is that you allow the Spirit of God to search out the deep things of Him, because no one knows the *Spirit of God except the Spirit of God*. So I asked myself the following question: Was He waiting for me to say, "Master, at your bidding, I will let down the nets*"?*

Well, that is what I'm doing now! When you let down your nets, you're bound to catch something. What do I want to catch? This book is my net and I'm dropping it into the deep. The "deep" to me entails growing deeper in maturity in Him, and for non-believers to want to know God and realize how much He loves them. There is no limit to the depth we can go with Him.

In 2009, I received a word from the Lord, "*Don't go wide, go deep.*" I pondered this word many times. I asked the Lord for more understanding. He said, "*If you go wide in the things of Me, you will not be able to go deep.*" On the other hand, if I go deep, I will automatically then go wide in my depth and understanding. There is so much depth in the Word of God that it takes a **searching spirit and soul** to comprehend its revelatory meaning. There are *blessings of the deep* spoken of in Genesis 49:25. As you read the following chapter, let's claim these blessings for ourselves. It only took me three years to move on this meditative thought, "**Launch Out**

Into the Deep." I may move slowly, but Jesus' disciples moved quickly. I love the way Jesus called the disciples and they dropped what they were doing and followed Him.

The Miraculous

Let's go to Luke 5:4: *The miraculous catching of fish.* Jesus was teaching and a multitude was gathering about Him to hear the Word of God. As Jesus was standing by the Lake of Gennesaret, He saw two empty boats. The fishermen that owned the boats were washing their nets. Jesus climbed into Simon's boat and asked him to move a little away from the shore (or land). He then began to teach the people from the boat.

As Jesus taught, the anointing flowed. Always remember, there is an anointing on Jesus and His word as He speaks. One can just imagine the spiritual energy that was being released from Christ and His word. The whole crowd must have been charged with the electricity of Christ's glory.

When Jesus was through teaching, He said to Simon, "*Launch out into the deep and let down your nets for a catch.*"

Simon, like me, did not get it at the first command. He says, "I have been at this all night and have caught nothing." Then he states, "*at your word,* I will release my nets." (Has God released a word to you?) At that time, nets were bell-shaped with lead weights placed around the edges to weigh down the nets so they could lay flat on the water. The weights would cause the nets to go to the bottom and cover the fish. The fisherman would then pull a cord and gather the fish in the net. I, not being a fisherman, thought this was an amazing way to catch fish.

Simon released the nets and caught so many fish that their nets began to tear. They signaled for help. They filled two boats and the two boats began to sink. All were astonished at the amount of fish that were taken. (Luke 5:7)

And here is the big anointed word that Jesus spoke to Simon, "*Do not be afraid, from now on you will catch men.*" (Luke 5:9) Jesus said to Peter and Andrew as they cast a net into the sea, "F*ollow me and I will make you fishers of men.*" (Matthew 4:19)

What kind of nets such as words, writings, teachings, prayer, prophesy, and ministry are we releasing to catch people for the Kingdom of Heaven? One of my nets is this book. Speaking of a book reminds me of King David's writings in the book of Psalms.

David's Anointing

One of the greatest anointed writers in the Old Testament was David. He ministered and sent out a net that is probably the biggest people catch for the Kingdom of Heaven. **David launched out into the deep when he wrote the Psalms**. I believe David was in a deep spiritual dimension in the Lord when writing the Psalms where he agonized on his own behalf and for others.

David blazed a spiritual path that we could enter into. Have we not realized, or rather have we not gotten the revelation, or the depth, that David entered to bring forth the Psalms for us? God revealed these Psalms to David to be written for us by His Spirit. *...For the spirit searcheth all things, yea, the deep things of God.* (I Corinthians 2:10) David let the spirit of the Lord search out the depth of him, and then he wrote about it. David stated in II Samuel 23:2, "the spirit of the Lord spoke by me, And His word was on my tongue." Read David's Psalm of thanksgiving in II Samuel 22.

Proverbs 20:27 states, *the spirit of man is the candle of the Lord that searches out all the inward parts of the belly.* The Lord uses our own spirit (just as he did David's) as the Holy Spirit's candle to search out truth in our inward parts to bring truth to the very core of our being. David had to **launch out into the deep in the Lord to accomplish this**.

I can almost feel David's depth of agony when he wrote "*deep calleth unto deep at the noise of the waterfalls: all thy waves and thy billows are gone over me.*" (Psalms 42:7). Sounds like depression to me. David spoke of his enemy's oppressing him and his soul being cast down. He rose up from that depth and said, *my hope is in God and I will praise Him*. He is the help of my countenance. **Shall we say that David knew how to go to the deep?** David's writings inspire me because the Lord said David was a man after God's own heart. David is not the only one who can have a heart after God. We can examine our own hearts and follow David's example when he became the Lord's beloved.

How Deep Is Deep?

There is a depth in the Lord that we need to search out. I looked up the word depth in New Webster Dictionary and one of the meanings was "situated far down from the surface." My mind wanders to a thought that we need to be more than surface Christians and go

to a new depth in Him. There were many other defini-
tions to the words deep and depth; some applied, some
did not. Questions we might ask ourselves:

What is deep?
Where is the deep?
Where do I let my nets down?
What am I supposed to catch?

I envision the deep as losing myself totally in
Jesus. Where? In my sphere of influence, in the territory that has been given to me and where I'm being
led. What is the catch? I see the catch as being people,
life words and truth – my people perish for lack of
knowledge. I am to help bring life, truth and knowledge to God's chosen people. Who, what people?
Those locked into captivity, by a prison of their own
making or by others that have put them in bondage.

> Isaiah 61 states, *the Spirit of the Lord
> anoints us to preach to the poor, heal
> the brokenhearted, declare liberty to
> the captives, open prison doors to
> those who are bound, and to comfort
> all who mourn.*

How do we know and understand these things of God? Scripture tells us *But God has revealed them to us through His Spirit. For the spirit searches all things, yes the deep things of God.* (I Corinthians 2:10-12). The next scripture in Chapter 2 explains that when we receive the Spirit of God, we know these **deep things that are freely given to us by God.** In this same chapter, scripture releases one of the deeper profound words of Paul:

> *But it is written: Eye has not seen nor ear heard, nor have entered Into the heart of man the things which God has prepared for Those who love Him.*

What does the above scripture mean to me? I have not even begun to know the depths of the love God has for me. My eyes can't see, nor my ears hear, and my heart often has a hard time receiving the things God has prepared for me. The deep longing of my soul is to go to the depth of His love. This is where He wants to take me. One of those deeper places that I know He wants to take me is His Rest.

God's Rest

God's rest is when you have **Launched Out Into the Deep** and you're in waters over your head. It is when you glide into that place where you cease from your own efforts and God takes over. The word states:

> *For he that hath entered into His rest has himself also ceased from His works as God did from His.*

Our Lord has **reserved a place of rest** for each of us through every promise and provision He has bequeathed to us. It is necessary to know what those stated inheritances are. Believe me, time and space will not permit me to write about all God's promises for us. This will be your task and as you do this, you will go into a new depth with Him. Listen up! Do you have any obstacles that keep you from truly being able to retreat to a place of rest in the Lord? A place that you have never been before, that lets you truly be with Him? A place where there are no obstacles or hindrances? A place where you can sit in heavenly places with Him?

Isn't God good to provide a place where we can remove the obstacles of yesterday (the past) to bring us into the present, and be able to take our authority over anything that would hinder our relationship with Him? In order to have the kind of relationship we want with God and others, we need to be free to voice what is deep in our hearts and minds. Also, we need environments (of all kinds) that will help us voice what is inside. Our environments, (meaning where we are and what is around us) often determine our freedom of total expression, spirit, soul and body.

Why do we need to voice what is inside us? What we see on the outside of us is temporary. However, what happens on the inside of us is eternal. We tend to focus on the things we can see and hold this in evidence for truth. Launching out moves us into an eternal depth.

Launch Out

Launching out into the deep is plunging in to the depth of truth and discernment that God opens up for us. The sons of Issachar (I Chronicles 12:32) had understanding of the times to know what Israel ought to do. That means we too can have understanding of our times.

This reminds me of a scripture in Isaiah 9:2, *The people who walked in darkness have seen a great light.* We are walking in more light now than ever before. When we grow deeper in the Lord, the darkness around us diminishes and we walk in His light. **In His light, we are in His rest.** Resting in Him is when we have truly **launched out into the deep** because our faith and trust is in the **depth of Him.**

My goal in writing this chapter is to stimulate Christians to go deeper into the love of the Lord, and also to be strengthened so they will not be "double minded" and unstable in their journey with Him (James 1:8). Being double minded seems to be a big problem in Christian maturity. For example, Satan is a master at putting doubt and unbelief in our minds, thus, causing us to second guess our choices and decisions, which result in self-doubt and double mindedness in the things of the Lord.

I am again reminded of all David's writings and his journey *from the depths of despair to the height of victory.* He is a shining example of the victory we can have in our lives.

Reflections

When the Holy Spirit brought my attention to Luke 5:4 many years ago and many other times through the years. I began a journey and a path that prepared me for *such a time as this*. What is *such a time as this* for me and for you? Deuteronomy 30:14 tells us "*but the word is very near you in your mouth and in your heart that you may do it.*" *Selah!* What a promise. He is in my heart and on the tip of my tongue, to do His word.

My thought is **the depth we're willing to go with the Lord, is the depth of the degree of anointing we will walk in. How deep are we willing to go to see or be in God's glory and to know His presence**?

Meditative Prayer

How can I know Him and love Him with the depth that I want to and the depth He wants me to unless I study His word, read His mind, know His heart. Then study his covenants, statues, and laws. In other words, study His nature, His characteristics.

Who is this awesome God who made the ultimate sacrifice for me to live eternally with Him? What provisions has He made that I may keep His covenant statutes and laws, and not feel like He is controlling me and making demands that I think (in my mind) are unreasonable for such a time as this?

It is all about love. What do I love? What am I committed to out of love, not fear? I must make the cross, the blood and Christ's sacrifice a very personal thing that He did for me personally – not mankind – but for me personally. I need to know I'm like the first Adam and that He has made a special provision for me to have complete restoration and a special walk, and talk, and time with Him daily like Adam did.

His (Christ's) resurrection is my resurrection into the new dimension that Christ has made a provision for. He said we could sit in heavenly places with Him and this is what I intend to do!!!

Anita

Abiding Rest
Scriptures to Mediate On

Leviticus 23.3 - *Six days shall work be done; but on the seventh day is a sabbath of solemn rest, a holy convocation; you shall do no work.*

Psalms 62.1 - *For God alone my soul waits in silence.*

Ecclesiastes 4.6 - *Better is a handful of quietness than two hands full of toil.*

Isaiah 28.12 - *Give rest to the weary.*

Isaiah 30.15 - *For thus says the Lord God, the Holy One of Israel, 'In returning and rest you shall be saved.'*

Jeremiah 6.16 - *Thus says the Lord:*
'Stand by the roads, and look,
And ask for the ancient paths,
Where the good way is; and walk in it,
And find rest for your souls.'

Matthew 11.28-30 - *Come to me, all who labour and are heavy laden, and I will give you rest. Take my yoke upon you, and learn from me; for I am gentle and lowly in heart, and you will find rest for your souls. For My yoke is easy, and my burden is light.*

Hebrews 4.9-11 - *So then, there remains a sabbath rest for the people of God; for whoever enters God's rest also ceases from his labours as God did from His. Let us therefore strive to enter that rest.*

Revelation 14.13 - *Blessed are the dead who die in the Lord henceforth. 'Blessed indeed,' says the Spirit, 'that they may rest from their labours, for their deeds follow them!'*

I will be in agreement with you when you speak out this **Prayer for Deep and Secret things of the Lord**.

Prayer for Deep and Secret Things of the Lord

Father, I want to make myself available to the Holy Spirit for His restorative work. Daniel 2:22 says: *"He reveals the deep and secret things. He knows what is in the darkness and the light dwells with Him."*

Father, reveal the deep and secret things within me. You know what is in darkness, so take all the dark areas out of me and bring me into the marvelous light of Christ that brings health, healing and wholeness.

Amen

Declarations

I declare God's anointing will be upon me in the depth of His catches.

I declare I will know and understand what "Deep calls to deep" means to God.

I declare I am in the boat with Christ and He is at the helm.

I declare I abide in Christ and Christ abides in me. This is my revelation of depth.

I declare I will not be double-minded and unstable in my Christian journey.

I declare that I will "Launch out into the deep" and let my nets down for a catch. Meaning what God directs me to do.

Selah!

My blessings to you as you read and meditate on the following chapters.

Anita

No Body's Home

A real healing occurs when you do the right thing in the worst of circumstances.

– Anita Mason 05/09/2000

A few months ago I gave a teaching on intimacy. It was obvious as I began to go deeper into my subject that several of the attendees were getting uncomfortable. I was aware that this might be a difficult topic for some. Hey, it was a difficult teaching for me also.

However, **Intimacy** is not the only issue I want to write about. The other two issues are **Love** and **Mindlessness**. These topics can become endless in content and research. It is not my intent to go that deep. My intent is to give a basic understanding of how intimacy, unhealthy love and mindlessness keep us from connecting with one another in wholesome healthy relationships.

Let's begin with intimacy. First of all, intimacy is not an alternate word for sex. One of the simplest explanations for intimacy is **giving of myself and receiving from another.** This sounds simplistic, however, in reality when in a relationship, one is giving and the other is taking. I Cor. 14:40 states, *Let all things be done decently and in order.* This scripture speaks that there is an appropriate balance in everything. Giving and receiving is one of the most important and honoring principles in any relationship.

Speaking of relationships, what attracts one person to another? In marital therapy it has been noted that the qualities inhibited by partners, that attracted them to each other, are often the same ones that are identified that caused conflict later in the relationship. These qualities that attracted us to our partners, after a period of time, become obvious as difficult personality traits that became problematic and negative.

I chose the topic **"No Body's Home"** to describe many difficult adjustments in relationships. After the honeymoon stage of any relationship it often moves into **mindlessness.** Meaning the body is present, but emotionally (and often mentally) the person is not there. Is this an indicator that love for the partner is not there? Was intimacy lacking? Not necessarily, maybe prior intimacy faded away.

What is Love?

There are many kinds of love. We usually love someone with the same measure of love that was given to us. The person giving love usually thinks they love deeply, even when it's an elusive surface love.

Let's examine **"What Is Love"**. What makes us loveable to someone else? Is love and intimacy the same emotion? Not necessarily. The ability to experience love, to give and receive this sensuous, yet most basic of all emotions, is apparently a learned characteristic that is developed in stages from infancy to adulthood. Also, the ability to feel and express love is learned through early development and conditioning.

If our early conditioning is biblically based we are taught that our greatest commandment is to love God and one another, Matthew 22:37-40. Also in Romans 13:8 *Love worketh no ill to his neighbor*. We are given this basic Christian teaching and then the **"cares of the world"** engulf us and at some point in our lives, we end up going back and "doing our first works over again."

What does this mean? At some point in our Christian walk, God's basic principles are lost and we have to go back and find our **"first love"** again, meaning Christ. In our early development the emotion of love is first experienced in infancy. Our nurturing is primarily given from our mothers.

Infants who are held and nurtured identify themselves as special and worthy of love. This is how they learn to love themselves – and others. Apparently, an infant must have this experience of themselves as a **"beloved infant"** before they can experience love in relation to another. Persons who lack this initial experience of love will, as they mature, try to compensate for their lack of self-love by demonstrating a self-centeredness, meaning, **perceiving others chiefly in terms of their usefulness and by manipulating them for personal gain.** God's Word changes all this. *Therefore if anyone is in Christ, he is a new creation; old things have passed away; behold all things have become new.* (II Cor. 5)

Love shares many of the aspects of caring, such as affection, respect, and admiration, but other aspects of love are different than liking. Love is also **attachment or bonding** to the other that creates a very strong feeling of comfort or satisfaction when the significant other person is present.

Acute feelings of longing or depression known as "**separation distress**" or often called **"separation anxiety"** occur when the other is neither present nor accessible.

Reality is that attachment is the last characteristic of love to fade away, occurring long after aspects such as attraction, respect, and trust have vanished. **Mature love is when we desire greater satisfaction from providing nurture than from receiving it**. Also, mature love means giving when one is not expecting something in return. It is not conditional. We need to learn that love is nurturing, unconditional, and it is given freely, with no strings attached.

I discovered many of the persons I have counseled with do not know what genuine love is. For many, love is conditional. For example, this thought is prevalent; I will continue to love you if you meet all my needs or expectations. And long after the dream that most of us have had fades, there is left a spouse or significant other who blames the other for not living up to their unrealistic expectation. Only **attachment remains**, but often the wrong kind of attachment. It is not a healthy attachment that identifies with love and bonding. This type of attachment is called **dependent, co-dependent, or addictive.**

Earlier in my profession, I heard the following illustration: the sexual addict turns on, the romance addict moves on, and the relationship addict holds on.

We need to be loved in order to know how to love; we have to be bonded with loved ones in order to bond naturally with others. **The bottom line is if we teach our children to give and receive love in the developmental years, this will allow them to see themselves** as valued and loved.

Intimacy

Speaking of valued and loved, King Solomon takes us on a deep intimate journey in *Song of Solomon*. I cannot read this book without feeling like I have walked into someone's private space. This chapter of the Bible is tender, loving, searching and full of spiritual intimacy.

Relationships, (referring to the Shulamite woman and her beloved), in the *Song of Solomon* appears to be a metaphor describing or illustrating Christ's passionate love for His bride, the Church. The Holy Spirit inspired the creation of these biblical characters in *Song of Solomon* to underscore the dignity of love in marriage. **True intimate love can be pure, sanctified and full of intimate wonder.**

All of us have the ability to learn how to be appropriately intimate with others. The first requirement is to have an intimate relationship with ourselves.

How do we become intimate with ourselves? We need to discover who we are. What we want and what we don't want. This requires being aware of what emotions we are experiencing at any given moment when we are hurt, angry, upset, fearful, sad, happy, and even peaceful. Another important requirement is to love ourselves with the same love Christ has for us. The parts of us we reject or hate will be the parts that God is lovingly healing. It's not wisdom to hate any part of God's creation. Remember, we are God's Intimate creation. His Word states, *We are fearfully and wonderfully made*. (Psalm 139:14)

When I am able to define my own emotions, I will be capable of loving someone else without losing myself in them. Having good boundaries and defining who I am from others, is the first key to healthy mature intimacy.

To understand why intimacy is so difficult for most of us, it would be beneficial to examine early family messages. I challenge you to do this regarding sexuality/intimacy. This fact remains, sex is not intimacy and intimacy is not sex. We all need intimate relationships with significant others in order to know the difference between intimacy and sex. How do we differentiate between sex and intimacy? We experience this through love, sharing our dreams, our success and failures, and openly discussing our disappointments. Trust is another important factor in intimacy. Without trust in our relationships, intimacy cannot be built.

It is imperative that we find safe places and safe people to help us build trust. Also to unravel emotional damage and heal when we lack nurturing (meaning some form of meaningful touch). I equate intimacy and nurture as one and the same (can't have one without the other). God created our skin to hunger for touch. Skin hunger is quickened by touching, soothing, and loving. This is what gives us a sense of life. Many people starve from skin hunger. Touching is a form of healing. Touch heals us spiritually, physically, and emotionally. When we mature and understand what the meaning of intimacy really is, then skin hunger will not be the upmost **superficial** connection that we seek.

In the *Book of Solomon*, the Shulamite woman was not seeking just touch from her beloved; she was passionately seeking his love. My thought is, the *Song of Solomon* is about the Shulamite maiden's love for Solomon. She trusted his deep emotional commitment to her as his forth-coming bride. This message of love is what Christ wanted us to comprehend as His bride. We can trust Him with every facet of our lives. **Trust, love, honesty, commitment and liberty** are all the basic ingredients for true and unleavened intimacy. When we trust Christ, we are able to experience life and be present with ourselves and others, not moving through life **mindless**.

Mindlessness

What is mindless? This is where we're on automatic pilot and not fully present in what we are doing. In other words, the body is in one place and the mind in another. This also keeps us from loving fully as we were created to do. Does this description describe anyone in particular?

When we do not embrace and do not know how to stay in the present moment, I call this mindlessness, (moving through life and experiences not connected to anything or anybody). Remember, **"just because your living does not mean you gotta life."** (quote Anita)

The reason I chose **"No Body's Home"** for this chapter is for this very reason. Many people are living, but they don't embrace life. Embracing life is being present with it, feeling it, knowing you're alive, and your spirit being quickened when connecting with others.

I have counseled and ministered to numerous people that their body is there with me, but the rest of them is not present. For a true healing to occur, all parts of our spirit, soul and body need to be equally alive. To be alive means to be fully awake. Being fully awake is to **"stir up or rouse one's self"**. This word **awake** is found 80 times in the Hebrew Old Testament. In Isaiah 52:1 God declares "*AWAKE, AWAKE; put on thy strength O Zion.*" We need this awakening strength.

Our God wants us awake and alive. He does not want our spirits in a state of slumber. Biblically, this is how God explains slumber, "*God has given them the spirit of stuper, Eyes that they should not see And ears that they should not hear, to this very day.*" (Romans 11:8)

God's explanation of spiritual slumber reminds me of an incident in the New Testament. It is called **"The Walk to Emmaus"**. Shortly after Christ had arisen from the sepulcher, two men were walking from Emmaus to Jerusalem. (This is approximately 7 miles from Jerusalem.) They were discussing what had happened with Jesus. . (Luke 24:15)

One of the men, named Cleopas, began to tell Jesus of all the events that had happened with this mighty prophet, and today is the third day since His death. They continued to share with Jesus that a certain woman reported His body was gone and a vision with angels was present, stated He was alive. (Luke 24:16)

My thought is **"nobody"** was home spiritually with these two men. Was their spirit in a state of slumber? They did not know nor discern that their Savior was walking along side of them. How many of us have encountered Jesus' presence and did not acknowledge that He was walking along side of us? Are we able to discern when our spirits may be in a state of slumber?

Another example is driving a car. When driving, many eat and drink, text, read, talk on the phone, listen to music, even write when possible. You are able to do all these things and drive the car without thinking. You're on **automatic pilot**, often driving mindlessly.

When you are driving mindlessly, you are not as aware of the blind spots as you should be. And often not continuing to check the blind spots, especially on the right side of the car. This could cause disastrous situations. Could this same principle of not being aware of spiritual blind spots lead you into a spiritual disaster? Mindless driving is what causes accidents. By the way, I had one of those mindless driving accidents last year. Mindless driving is one of my comparisons for mindless spirituality.

Often, Christians believe it is not necessary to use their minds to navigate their spirituality. The Bible tells us to be **renewed in the spirit of your mind** (Ephesians 4:23). This helps us to understand mindless Christianity and mindless spirituality that will lead us into deception and religiosity. Religiosity often happens when someone is "piggy backing" on someone else's spiritual beliefs and using them as their own to gain religious power and control over others. They do not own anything spiritually; they just take, borrow or steal from others. **Keep this thought in mind, if you don't own something you can't give it away**.

One thing is certain, Satan owns evil. He comes to steal, kill and destroy. He gives evil away to whomever is willing to receive it. We do not often consciously choose to receive anything from the evil one. However, if I surround myself with mindless, low energy listless people, I will become like the people I hang around with. I will be vulnerable to receive from this association the characteristics of those I'm with. This is called **Transference of Spirit**. Many persons and situations influence our lives by immature persuasive thoughts that often lead us in sin or unbelief. The Bible tells us to take heed of an evil heart of unbelief. (Hebrews 3:12)

I often challenge myself to be aware of how I entertain thoughts that steal my ability to stay focused in the present. This state of living on automatic pilot must be challenged for me to be free and become present in every moment of my life.

It is my responsibility to be mindfully aware of my emotions, physical distress, and interpersonal relationships. This is what I call wisdom.

Wisdom begets wisdom. The wisdom in Proverbs searches out that deep place within us that creates our thoughts. When these thoughts are brought forth they produce mature thinking. It is impossible to read and meditate on God's Word without it infiltrating every cell of our body. This in turn causes a positive chemical reaction at a cellular level, impacting our emotional and spiritual growth.

Here is a life prescription for you that I have determined to live by the past twenty-five years of my life. I have shared and ministered these principles to many people.

1. **Stay in the present**
2. **Feel your feelings**
3. **Take downtime**
4. **Listen to your body**

I pray that you will be fully aware of times you may be mindless or on "automatic pilot," navigating through life. Be blessed with these activations.

Prepare for War Against Mindlesness

- "Lord, how do I get my heart ready for war?"
- Do I call upon the Lord? Psalms 116:1
- Have I made any vows to the Lord that I haven't kept? Psalms 116:14, 18-19
- Do I delight greatly in His commandments? Psalms 112:1
- Do I fear the Lord? Psalms 112:1
- Have I made the decision to praise the Lord with my whole heart? Psalms 111:1
- Have I acknowledged (received) the Lord's love because He has heard my voice and supplication? Psalms 116
- Have I stated to the Lord with my whole heart, have I sought you? Psalms 119:10

Mindless Declarations

- I declare I choose to not be mindless.
- I declare I will war against a worldly mindset.
- I declare I will keep my heart open to Your Word.
- I declare your thoughts will live and rule in my thinking and being.
- I declare a new found love to know and understand true spiritual intimacy.
- I declare I will be mindful of all the things the Lord is teaching me.

Ending Mindlessness

Lord Jesus, I don't want to be mindless. I want your mind to be within me. Let your thoughts live and rule in all my thinking and being.

I don't want my worldly knowledge; I want your truth in my inward parts. Purge my mind according to Your Word.

Open your Word to my heart daily, upsetting and replacing whatever the world has entangled within me.

Bring my mindlessness to death in all its ways of keeping me from my feelings and not allowing me to stay in the present with myself and others.

Lord, I give you all the thanks for healing my thoughts and my mind as I walk out of mindlessness to be present with You and others.

Your Loving Servant

Jacob's Limp, Part I

In our wilderness are we bearing fruit? Are you allowing others – instead of God to prune you?

– Anita Mason

One of the most famous (and to me fascinating) accounts of God's multiplication of grace is found in Genesis 32:24. An angel of the Lord came to Jacob while he was at Peniel (which means face of God). *He was to have a face to face encounter with God.* Jacob, whose name means "*usurper*" (rightfully so), *received his limp at the hand of the Lord.*

Jacob had sent his wives, servants, and sons to go before him, and he stayed behind. I believe Jacob stayed behind to seek the Lord. The scriptures state a man came and wrestled all night until the "*breaking of the day*" with Jacob (Genesis 22:24).

The man saw that Jacob was not giving up in the wrestling match and that Jacob could hold his own with him. All I can say is that Jacob must have been in very good physical condition because *the Lord did allow him to prevail*.

As I meditated on this God ordered incident, (evidently mentally and emotionally and definitely physically), Jacob was ready to have some kind of encounter with the Lord. Why else would Jacob stay behind (alone) and send family, servants, and possessions on ahead of him? He wanted the blessing. I'm sure he did not realize what he was going to have to go through to get that blessing, although Jacob knew he had an inherited blessing. How did Jacob know about his blessing? Because prior to his life with Rebecca, Jacob had lied to obtain his own father's (Abraham's) blessing. *He deceived his father, and his father-in-law deceived him. Can you see the law of sowing and reaping exhibited here?*

Jacob's Trauma

It must have been Jacob's *seasoned season* to fulfill God's covenant promises handed down through Grandfather Abraham to him. Prior to Jacob's encounter with the Angel of the Lord Jesus, *Jacob experienced trauma at the hand of his father-in-law—Laban*.

Jacob served Laban for 14 years before he could marry the love of his life, Rachael. Then his beloved wife was not able to conceive. She was childless, like Jacob's mother Rebecca. *Did you notice there is a definite family pattern (curse) being revealed here?* Jacob's connection with Laban involved much trauma for him. He endured being *deceived, betrayed, wounded,* and *mentally* and *emotionally* violated by his father-in-law. He was basically being held in bondage by Laban.

Genesis 31 tells the story of Jacob's flight with family, cattle, and belongings from Laban's abusive control over him and his family. This was just prior to Jacob's traumatic all-night encounter with the Angel of the Lord. As a result, his new name was a reminder of his new relationship with the Lord. He would no longer be *Jacob the upsurfer* but *Israel the prevailer*. Jacobs name also means *Penial—Place of God*.

Jacob must have sensed his time to *recover* his blessing from the Lord because of his ancestors covenant with *Yahweh*.

Jacob's Limp

Well, Jacob received alright; he received a pronounced limp. The man who he wrestled with touched the hollow of his thigh, and Jacob's thigh was put out of joint. (Genesis 22:25) Basically, Jacob's hip was injured so that it would be a constant reminder that he would not be walking through the rest of his life in his own strength but in the dependence and strength of the Lord.

When he stopped wrestling with the Angel of the Lord and *held on in desperate determination, Jacob received the blessing of the Lord, and his life was literally changed from his own independence to God's dependence.* To me, this God encounter is a way of letting us realize that we must have our own type of contact with the Lord. It may not always be a physical wrestling. *It is often an emotional, mental, or spiritual war we have with ourselves and* others as well as powers and principalities.

At this time, we need to get alone and call upon the Lord. We may have to *wrestle* all night in prayers and intercession to have the Lord touch us, and let that touch be a reminder that God met us at our point of need.

Just as he did with Jacob, this encounter that Jacob went through and "*prevailed*" is what I think is our reminder that *we all have a limp of some sort. I see this limp as a weakness that will keep us dependent on God for all our provisions that he has covenanted to us.*

A covenant reminder of God's guidance and blessings is in Zechariah 4:6, "*Not by night, nor by power, but by my spirit, saith the Lord of Hosts*".

With this promise, every wound, all the trauma (which we all experience at some time through our journey of life), even powers and principalities that we encounter, our loving *Father will walk through with us.* We may come through trials and tribulations with a limp, but we will come out victoriously. *We need to have our own face to face encounter with God.* I am now meditating and writing on a New Testament account of *another type of limp (internal)* that Peter the Apostle must have felt. Next is Peter's Message.

Prayer and activation will be at the end of Part II.

Peter's Limp, Part II

How can I build deeper spiritual character that will sustain me in trying times?

– Anita Mason

Have you ever just sat and thought, or rather meditated, on Peter's writings? The great Peter who stated *"Even if I have to die with you, I will not deny you"* (Matthew 26:35). In Matthew 26:34, Jesus says *"Assuredly, I say to you that this night before the rooster crows, you will deny me three times."* I often think about Peter's determination to show his loyalty to his master Jesus, and then later, when his life was at stake, he denied Christ just like Christ said he would.

This biblical example of a false sense of confidence, often called self-righteousness, reveals our weaknesses in our humanity. I believe the very sense of betrayal that Peter had to walk through is one of the main reasons Peter wrote the warnings in II Peter. This betrayal is a heartache that I believe Peter felt the remainder of his life.

Where Is Your Limp?

When I think of a lifetime of living with some type of pain, trauma, or infirmity, my mind remembers Paul. He had a limp because of some kind of infirmity.

I have thought much about Paul and his limp, and it is my belief that we all have a limp. We all have something in our lives that causes us to limp, something that we must seek Christ to overcome. That limp is a reminder we can't go anywhere without him. We must deal with it and allow Christ to walk out our limp with us.

It is safe to say *Peter's limp*, unlike Paul's, was his betrayal of his beloved savior. This is why I believe Peter had a passion to share with us the same grace and peace he knew we would need on our spiritual journeys. One of the greatest obstacles on our spiritual journey is self-condemnation. So he wrote in II Peter, *"Grace and Peace be multiplied to you in the Knowledge of God and of Jesus our Lord. As his divine power has given to us all things that pertain to life and godliness through the Knowledge of Him who called us by glory and virtue.*" We can be assured that Peter multiplied grace and peace in his writings to us because Christ gave these gifts to him after his betrayal.

Something before his betrayal of Christ gave Peter a false sense of security. II Peter was written by the Apostle Peter as a warning to keep us from falling into false doctrine. In this letter to us, he gives us *warnings* and *direct clues* on how to detect false teachers

This letter is written to the church at large, and Peter begins his script with God and Jesus Christ *imparting* their faith to us. As you read this, receive that *impartation of faith*. It is freely given.

He then *declares* a *multiplication* of Grace and Peace in the *knowledge* of God and our Savior Jesus Christ. How do we obtain this knowledge for the *multiplication* process to be activated in our spirits?

Line Upon Line

In the first chapter of II Peter, we are given distinct character qualities that we *must develop* through the precious promises that have been given to us. What are these character qualities; what are the precious promises? The scriptures give us a clear path to building spiritual character. While I was writing, I was meditating on what Peter wanted to transfer to us. Were these character building blocks meant to be built like a pyramid or even a *line upon line, precept upon precept?* (Isaiah 28:13)

Whatever or whichever, God has given to us His *divine power* (vs: 3) to accomplish all things that pertain to our life to *build godliness* in us through the *knowledge* of Him. The *knowledge* of Him is our key to the path that will build our spiritual character, which begins verse 5 of II Peter.

Peter begins with, *"But also for this very reason…"* Then I ask,"for what reason?" In verse four, Peter explains that through God's precious promises we will be *"partakers"* of His divine nature and will escape the corruption that is in the world. What does the word "partakers" imply? The American Heritage Dictionary states *"1.) To take part; participate. 2.) To take a portion."* Peter is saying that through God's promises we will not only have a part, but we will also have a **portion,** of His divine nature.

He then states what we have been given. He starts with faith and then adds the ingredients that God's promises have given to us. First, we have been given *diligence*, add to this *virtue* and continue to build on virtue; *knowledge,* add to knowledge *self-control;* to self-control, add *perseverance* (patience); to perseverance, add *godliness;* to godliness, add *brotherly kindness;* to brotherly kindness, add *love*. Last but not least is love. All these character ingredients will not come to *fruitation* without all of them being covered by love.

I envision the character building pyramid like this—*line upon line, precept upon precept*, beginning with the foundation of faith:

Love
Brotherly Kindness
Godliness
Perseverance
Self-Control
Knowledge
Virtue
Diligence
Faith

Here, again, are the precious promises that Peter spoke about in II Peter 1:4. He said that if we have these character qualities, we can be *partakers of His divine nature, escaping the corruption that is in this world that abides in our flesh* (paraphrased). God always provides an antidote.

This is the ultimate in God's promise to us. If we grow strong and spiritually enlarge ourselves in these godly characteristics, His promise is that we will not be *barren* or *unfruitful* in the knowledge of Christ (vs. 8 paraphrased). Note! It is *our* responsibility to embrace these characteristics and let them be rooted in us.

As we grow in the knowledge of Christ, we have it all. In fact, as these characteristics are manifest in us, we will maintain an *unquenchable passion* for Christ and His Kingdom. This reminds me of my number one principle that I strive to live in my life: *"But Seek ye first the Kingdom of God and His righteousness and all these things shall be added unto you."* (Matthew 6:33)

As for the meaning in II Peter, I recommend you read the whole chapter and let the Holy Spirit speak to you on how to determine what doctrinal error is and how to avoid it.

Selah! Anita

Spiritual Growth Declaration

- *I declare Diligence will be rooted and grounded in me.*
- *I declare Virtue will flow out of me.*
- *I decree Knowledge is my portion.*
- *I declare Self-Control will abide in me.*
- *I decree Perseverance will bring me to my destiny.*
- *I declare Godliness is my lifetime goal.*
- *I decree I will walk in Brotherly Kindness.*
- *I declare I am covered in God's Love, and He will bring forth all these character qualities in me.*

Meditate on this Prayer

Father God, thank you for Peter's message to the church. I receive the grace and peace that Peter imparted to me. Because of Your grace Lord, I'm able to move beyond my weaknesses. Reveal to me all the areas in my life where I may be limping spiritually. I lay all my weaknesses at Your feet Lord and ask that You strengthen and purify them. If I have a limp that is hindering me spiritually, reveal it to me so that Your grace and peace will guide me and heal my spirit, soul, and body. Thus, I will be able to fulfill my destiny the Father has purposed for me.

In Jesus' Name, Amen

God, What Are You Trying To Tell Me?

*When I stand before God at the end of
my life, I would hope that I would not
have a single bit of talent left but could
say, "I used everything you gave me."*
— Erma Bombeck (1927-1996)

Why did God make our lessons in life so *elusive* (or vague)? Many of our lessons are given to us by teachers and authority figures. I wonder how important the actual teaching of our authority figures, teachers, or mentors are for us to become *mature* Christian adults.

Could it be that it is more about relationships and building each other up than putting our mandates and perceptions on each other? More often, we haven't got our own issues dealt with. What is typical for many of us is that we perceive things through healed or unhealed perceptions. *If our perceptions are distorted, then what is being taught, advised, or ministered will have a degree of distortion when given to us.*

What is given is truth for them and, in turn, they perceive it to be truth for us. It is truth as they see it, not necessarily truth for us. Do we swallow all advice and teachings that our authority figures give us "*hook line and sinker?*" Or, are we mature enough to take whatever we need and just let the rest go?

Have I Arrived?

Maybe the following is not yet true for you, but it is for me. (Many of you can and will relate to what I am sharing.) Over the past 35 years, I have been to hundreds of workshops and conferences of all sorts. You name them, I have "been there, done that." I have gleaned much insight and knowledge as a result. However, with each place that I went with excitement and anticipation, I believed "*this will be the place*" where I will get just what I need, and then I'll find the Lord in a new way. No more struggles, no more down times, no more warring with myself to be what I thought was the overcoming spiritual Christian. "*I will have arrived.*" At each place, I would tell myself "*this will be the one.*" The next one, "*this will be the one*," and so on.

These opportunities to learn are great and also inspiring, but one cannot live off of them. When I returned from each event, the teaching somehow becomes *elusive* because I am letting someone else feed me my spiritual food and not learning to feed myself. We don't have to go all over the continent trying to *catch the Spirit.* We can grow in wisdom and mature daily if we don't just live off someone else's perceptions and interpretations of God's Word. When we do this, I call it walking in someone else's shadow or someone else's light (meaning other's revelations). In other words, feed yourself by reading and meditating on God's Word along with each event.

Maybe God made our authority figures' teachings somewhat elusive to us so we would get just enough teaching to ignite a fire in us to search Him and His Word out for our own personal growth. We also need to discern truth and distortion from error and false perceptions. *We are to desire truth in our inward parts* (Psalm 51:6). He also said the Holy Spirit would teach us (John 14:26). What does this mean? David stated in Psalm 51:10, "create in me a clean heart and renew a right spirit in me." David expected God to instruct him.

I John 4:6 says if we are of God, we hear him, if not of God, we will not hear Him, *"By this we know the spirit of truth and the spirit of error."* If we believe what the word says and, if we are passionately seeking the Lord and His truth, we will discern when distorted teaching is being fed to us.

Spiritual Food

We need gatherings, especially in the church, to build relationships for the edification, or lifting up, of each other and in the body of Christ. Hebrews 3:13 warns us to "***exhort*** one another daily, while it is called today." You'll also find in Romans 15:2, "Let each if us please his neighbors for his good, leading to ***edification***." This scripture is self-explanatory, isn't it? It is my understanding that the New Testament is all about how we are to relate to Christ and to each other. Thus, we are given explicit instructions on how to do this.

Wherever we go, whether it is a conference, a workshop, or the local church, we will hear other's perceptions of Christ and His Word. *Am I saying don't trust these places? God forbid, no!* Just don't be gullible and swallow anything and everything that is fed to you. Check and discern all things through the ***Holy Spirit*** and the ***Word*** which says, "Be diligent to present yourself approved to God, a worker who does not need to be ashamed, rightly ***dividing the word of truth***." (2 Timothy 2:15)

I John 2 explains all that I am trying to say. For example, verse 20 states that you have an anointing from the *Holy One,* and you know all things. The anointing that you received and that resides in you teaches you truth as you abide in Him (verse 27).

One of the ways that we will learn to walk in maturity is in our daily connection with significant others in our life. Why? Because our Christian character will be worked out in our relationships. In fact, nothing is ever accomplished in isolation. We must be in relationships in order to heal and to allow our issues to surface. It is not only a good thing, but a Godly thing, to be accountable to someone. Relationships accomplish this.

One of my favorite sayings that the Lord gave me fifteen years ago is *"Isolation breeds deception."* It is one of the principles that I share when teaching or counseling, meeting with individuals and/or groups. The word says when two walk together, one will hold the other up when needed. When the word states *"iron sharpens iron,"* I believe those sparks from the iron will be *discerning lights* that will touch us to help repair and heal all relationships.

Who is the Strongman?

For our relationships and other problematic issues to be healed, the Word says we must first *"Bind the strongman"* (Matthew 12:29). Who is the strongman? My perception is that it's an evil presence that keeps us in a type of bondage. In Matthew 12:25-29, Jesus is speaking to the Pharisees. He was reading their thoughts. Jesus told them that kingdoms, cities, and houses divided against themselves will not stand. **Take note, nothing divided against itself will stand.**

He then shares the principles of casting out demons by the Spirit of God. *He tells the Pharisees that before one can enter a strongman's house (a demonic stronghold-my perception) and take what belongs to you, you must first bind the strong man* and then your goods (anything valuable, physical, or spiritual) can be retrieved. Remember, Matthew says *first bind the strongman*. As we uncover lies that demonic forces tell us, the Holy Spirit will teach us to confront these lies by embracing God's truth. Truth exposes and binds the strongman.

I understand this portion of scripture is a bit hard to understand and to spiritually digest its meaning.

It appears that our lessons in life that are *elusive* slip away easily and need to be held onto like a rock until we learn from them what God is revealing to us. It is important to have teachers and authority figures in our Christian journey, but do not let them take the place of our *personal search of the scriptures* so that the *Spirit of Truth* will be active in us.

Last year, the most important three words I sensed the Lord telling me were to *Listen, Meditate,* and *Activate. Listen to hear* His voice guiding and directing me. *Meditate, soak in His word,* and confirm what I sense He is telling me. Then *Activate, move on what he is telling me.* This word from the Lord is one of the reasons for this book. I am *activating* what the Lord has directed me to do, *"write this book"*.

Here is a prayer to break free of deception that I have written just for you.

Breaking Strongholds of Deception

Father, I commit myself totally, spirit, soul, and body, to Your will.

Lord, any areas in which I have been deceived, believing the lie that I have a right to be anxious about most things—I renounce that lie and ask forgiveness for believing that lie. Now Lord, open my eyes to deception and anxiety that is not godly in my life.

Lord Jesus, break the stronghold of deception that hides fear within me. Break it right now, in Jesus' name. Lord Jesus, I come against that root of fear that is within me. I break its ruling power.

I renounce fear and all its associated demonic spirits attached to me. I command in the name of the Lord Jesus Christ that all fear depart from me, and I renounce and reject any counterfeit spirits that would remain to deceive me.

Thank you, Lord, for the delivering power of Your Blood and Your Saving Grace to heal me.

Let Your Healing Blood be upon me.

AMEN

I am ending this chapter with declarations and a meditative poem the Lord gave me in January of 2007.

Let's Declare What God is Telling Us

- *I declare my spiritual perception will not be distorted.*
- *I declare I will not presume I have arrived.*
- *I declare I will help God build His church on relationships.*
- *I declare I desire truth in my inward parts.*
- *I declare I will study to show myself approved to know the difference between truth and the spirit of error.*
- *I declare I will not allow isolation in me to breed deception.*
- *I declare when I bind the strongman he will not rule and reign in my life.*

Meditation

By the time I die, I'll know why I live.
And while I live, I'll learn how to die.
Because death is just my transition of life.
Put all this together and you have touched,
God's great Divine.
I'm off and in the running to live to the fullest,
This great life.
And when this journey is over
I'll transcend into God's light.
Peace is my heavenly vehicle,
Not by Power,
Nor by might.
For God is in the Throne Room,
Waiting for my life.

Selah, Anita

A Man of Vision

*Jeremiah 23:29 is not my word like a
fire says the Lord, And like a hammer
that breaks the rock in pieces.*

I am in love with the book of Isaiah. Is Isaiah my
favorite book of the Bible? I have several favorites, and Isaiah is one of them. There are so many
passages of scripture in Isaiah that I *"ooh"* and *"awe"*
over. As a result, I want to share some of these scriptures in this chapter.

I can't say I understand all that Isaiah is expressing,
but when I read certain scriptures, something in my
spirit leaps. (I think its truth in my inward parts.) My
mind wanders to the time that Mary and Elizabeth
met, and the baby (John) in Elizabeth's womb leaped
when meeting Mary carrying baby Jesus. (Luke 1:44)

I am purposely not going to share about all the
consequences of sin (basically judgment) that is
expressed in Isaiah; however, I do want to mention

some of the scriptures that have ministered to me over the years and still sustain me.

I began marking scriptures in my Bible in 1978. Since that time, I have purchased several new Bibles, and I find in each one I have continued to mark the same scriptures. I find this amazing because each time I read these same scriptures in another Bible, they quicken my spirit again, just like I'm reading the word for the first time. Isn't this amazing? This proves to me how timely and fresh God's word truly is.

Prophetic Authority

I am impressed *with the authority Isaiah* was given to make proclamations from God. Remember, God is no respecter of persons; I can have the same anointed authority as Isaiah. He received visions from God inspired by the Holy Spirit. He saw coming events in God's plan of salvation. Isaiah's name means "The Lord Saves." Isn't this just like our Father in Heaven to send a prophet that has a name that is an expression of His character—salvation? Isaiah also reported how Judah and Israel had broken their covenant with God and failed to acknowledge God as their source, resulting in Isaiah speaking of God's judgment for their idolatry.

In Isaiah, God spoke of the promises and provisions that He made to the people. Isaiah, as a true servant of the Lord, brought forth *God's unique character to His people*. Two main themes in Isaiah are *Man's foolishness of Idolatry* and *The Sovereignty of God*. These spiritual themes are prevalent throughout Isaiah.

Now, let's begin in the first chapter of Isaiah. It begins with a *proclamation for the heavens and earth to hear what God has spoken*. In verse 18 of the first chapter of Isaiah, a wooing, comforting word is spoken, "*come now and let us reason together,*" says the Lord. "*Though your sins are like scarlet, they shall be as white as snow; though they are red like crimson, they shall be as wool.*" Doesn't this sound like a loving God wanting to gather and cleanse His people?

I have found as I began writing my favorite scriptures in Isaiah that there are more scriptures than I am going to be able to share. So I will only touch on a few that I pray will be favorites for you also.

I get overwhelmed reading and meditating on my special enlightened scriptures in Isaiah. Bear with me. What I share will be just the tip of Isaiah's prophetic words. I will not be sharing the full context of the scriptures that I glean insight and often direction from. My prayer is that you look them up and let the Spirit of the Lord speak to you.

Seven Spirits of the Lord

As I share these scriptures in Isaiah, my prayer is that the Lord will "***Bind up His Testimony*** and ***Seal His laws*** within you" (Isaiah 8:16). Whenever I or my prayer team prays for others, we *seal* what we pray in Jesus name; we are just following Christ's example.

In Isaiah 11, the word states the *Seven Spirits of the Lord,* and they were manifested in Jesus:

Spirit of the Lord
Spirit of Wisdom
Spirit of Understanding
Spirit of Council
Spirit of Might
Spirit of Knowledge
Spirit of fear of the Lord

These same spiritual gifts and works Christ said we could also have, and greater, "because I go to My Father" (John 14:12).

Here is another strong word "***the Lord of Hosts***" gave to the people through Isaiah. "***Surely as I have thought, so it shall come to pass. And as I have*** *purposed it, so shall it stand*." God is sharing His nature with us. Whatever He thinks is happening and what He purposes is coming to pass. It is in the now, and it will stand.

What could one of God's purposes be? We want God's loving thoughts toward us, and His purposes for us to be fruitful and multiply. So when God thinks something, it is done; it is an instant happening.

One of the deeper insights I have received from the Lord is in Isaiah 28:9-13. Scripture asks who will He teach knowledge and who will understand the message? "Those just weaned from milk?" Here is the answer.

> *"For precept must be upon precept, precept upon precept, line upon line, line upon line. Here a little, there a little."*

In these scriptures, Isaiah is sharing with us how we mature in our understanding of God's message to us. As we grow in understanding and mature "*line upon line*" in our spiritual development (just like our natural developmental process), we will no longer be "babes" in Christ. In fact, we are building *revelation, insight,* and *wisdom* "*line upon line*" and "*precept upon precept.*" This will bring us into greater maturity as we apply God's word to our everyday life. (Isaiah 28:10)

Death Spirit?

In this same chapter (verse 28), after we're instructed how to grow up spiritually, another strong word is stated through Isaiah: "*we have made a covenant with death.*" Could we ever imagine that we could make a covenant (agreement) with death? Is there such a thing as a death spirit? It is my belief that there is such a spirit because of the many prayers I have prayed over people that have wanted to die and also prayers over self destructive behavior that could cause premature death.

I mention this because I work with a lot of persons who have shared their death wishes. Often, these oppressive and depressing thoughts of death are conscious and also unconscious. While ministering, we break all covenants (agreements) with a death spirit and call for life and "*life abundantly*".

It is rare for most people to understand that their wishes have caused them to make *agreements with death*. These death thoughts must be dealt with. God always brings forth what is hidden in the darkness. *A hidden truth* here is our death thoughts that can and often do produce premature death if not exposed. If we sow thoughts (consistently) of death, we will reap death in our lives. It could be *spiritual*, *emotional,* or *physical death*.

With death thoughts or wishes, we give the devil legal access to help propel us into death situations. Our covenants with God give us access to whatever God has for us. God has stated all through His message that he wants us to *claim our provided inheritance, prosper* in what we set our hands to, and *have abundant health, spirit, soul, and body*.

Well, this is a heavy topic that needs more revelation and insight. "*But, God*" is always faithful to pull us up out of anything that would be defeating for us. For example, Isaiah 41:10 gives us another promise:

> *"Fear not for I am with you; be not dismayed, for I am your God. I will strengthen you. Yes, I will help you. I will uphold you with My Righteous right hand"*.

This word from the Lord is a promise *He's declaring* to us. This scripture comes alive to me when I get in situations where I have no answers. Then

I am reminded of what God has provided for me. I was recently studying scriptures in Colossians when I received a deeper understanding (revelation) that Colossians 1:5 had for me. Grasp this: "*because of the hope which is laid up for you in heaven of which you heard before in the word of the truth of the gospel.*"

We actually have *hope stored up in heaven* for us that God provided when the truth of the gospel is received by us. Here is the concept: hope is already reserved for me in heaven. Our heavenly bank account has hope stored up for us. *Let's receive it.* We don't have to earn it; it's ours. Whether we receive it or not, the provision has been made. This was just a little side exhortation I wanted to share with you. Now, Isaiah has more to comfort us with.

The Comforter

The whole chapter of Isaiah 40 is a must read. It starts out with "*comfort, yes comfort my people.*" In this chapter, we are given many promises such as: our crooked places will be made straight and our rough places smoothed out. "*He will feed His flock like a shepherd.*" The last verse in this chapter is a kingdom promise that elevates us into a victorious place in Him:

"But those who wait on the Lord shall renew their strength; they shall mount up with wings like eagles. They shall run and not be weary, they shall walk and not faint."

This verse is one of the more well known verses in the Bible. This is one promise that will give us the peace and rest we need in perilous times. Continue with me for a couple more promises that God imparts to us in Isaiah. Another promise I often minister to others is:

"A bruised reed He will not break. And smoking flax he will not quench; He will bring forth justice for truth" *(Isaiah 42:3).*

He will not allow our bruises (or others that bruise us) to break us. As long as we have a flicker of life, He will not extinguish it. *Our Lord also challenges us to contend with Him. He tells us to state our case that we may be acquitted* (Isaiah 43:26). Our God is a just God. He will never take our voice away from us, and He gives us permission to put a demand upon Him, granted that demand must be presented in an honorable way. He listens and He responds.

Here is another confirmation of the above scripture that we have an audience with the Lord:

> *"Thus says the Lord, the Holy One of Israel, and His maker: Ask me of things to come concerning my sons; And concerning the works of my hands you command me. Isaiah 45:11*

When I meditate on this passage of scripture, it assures me that I have a voice and there is an open heaven and a throne room that we have access to. How many of us are aware of all the promises and provisions God has made for us to **"have life and have it abundantly"**?

Well, I for one take these promises and provisions seriously. Isn't the book of Isaiah fascinating as he shares with us *God's unique character*?

My Prophetic Prayer

Lord, I will not fear because I know You are with me. I will not be dismayed for I know You are my God. I am aware that You have chosen me and strengthened me. You are upholding me with Your Righteous Right Hand.

I will wait on You while You renew my strength. I shall run and not be weary; I will walk and faint not. I am able to do all these provisions because Your love and favor is upon me.

As a result, those who strive with me will perish. And those who contend with me and war against me shall be as nothing. You Lord, said "fear not, I will help you." This is my inherited promise and I receive it and ask You Lord to seal it within me.

Prayer from Isaiah 4
Amen

To Declare A Thing It's Established

- *I declare, Lord, I love Your word.*
- *I declare the Seven Spirits of the Lord will be established within me.*
- *I declare I will mature in God's principles "line upon line, precept upon precept".*
- *I declare that if I have made any covenant with a death spirit consciously or unconsciously, I renounce it and call that agreement null and void.*
- *I declare I have abundant health spirit, soul, and body.*
- *I declare I will fear not because I know You are with me to strengthen me and uphold me with Your Righteous Right Hand.*
- *I declare my goal is to learn more about God's unique character.*

Amen

Good Medicine

Prayer is the only thing that one can
say or do that takes us into yesterday,
keeps us in the present and propels us
into the future.

– Anita Mason 2/23/05

I have been shuffling through all my prayer journals and special articles that I have saved (for such a time as this). There is no doubt that I am not going to be able to share all that I have found. I have found not only invaluable material, but also many treasures that have helped build a strong foundation in my faith.

I'm holding in my hand (11-29-11) an awesome article that I saved. It continues to fulfill my expectation of how God encourages us in every aspect of life, beginning with prayer. This article is called *"Why Prayer Could Be Good Medicine"* by Diane Hales. This article came out of the Sunday morning Parade,

March 23, 2003. It gives valuable information on the research that explores the connection between biology and prayer that was once considered "*scientific heresy.*" Boy, have we come a long way since 2003. In other words, we're not rejecting scientific data like we have in the past. This is a sure sign of the revealed knowledge that the Lord is rapidly releasing.

Back to prayer being "*Good Medicine*". The article states "medical acceptance has grown along with solid scientific data on our prayers impact." Dr. Dale Matthews adds that he estimates that about 75% of studies on spirituality have confirmed health benefits. He states, "*If prayer were available in pill form, no pharmacy could stock enough of it.*" We have something better than a pill; we have the **word, promises,** and the **provisions of the Holy Spirit.**

In this same article, Dr. Harold Koenig, Director of Duke University's center that studies religion/ spiritually and health, writes about prayer. "**It boosts morale, lowers agitation, loneliness, life dissatisfaction, and enhances the ability to cope in men, women, the elderly, the young, the healthy and the sick. The article further stated "prayer and faith speeded recovery in illnesses ranging from depression to stroke to heart attack".**

A God Particle

The sciences are actually (positively) responding to the scientific research and studies that are confirming God's existence. In April of 2008, an article came out in print that stated "Scientists almost certain '*God particle*' will be found soon." My apologies, I retrieved the article, but I failed to write out what magazine I found it in.

"Geneva (AP) – the father of a theoretical sub-atomic particle dubbed, 'The God particle', says he's almost sure it will be confirmed in the next year in a race between powerful research equipment in the United States and Europe". This is a sophisticated technical article that brags of a $2 billion Large Hadrons Collider operating in a laboratory for physics.

Comments on this subject will be brief because of my lack of knowledge about this sophisticated equipment. These Collider scientists hope it will enable them to study particles and forces *yet unobserved*. Much is said in the Bible about the unseen world.

This is exciting news when "calling those things naught as though they are." Leon Lederman has a theory that "the '*God Particle*' discovery could unify understanding of particle physics and help humans *know the mind of God.*" (Who can know the mind of God?) My thought is that we continually pray to know the mind of Christ and heart of the Father and search Him out. Scientist's are at least searching for proof of the existence of God while we as Christians know the mind of God through His word.

Wonderfully & Fearfully Made

More confirmation confirming the existence of God is found in the *quantum* theories about our cell structure that research has scientifically proven. The researcher's that I gather my information from are Christians, and they credit God with their insight— especially when they are confirming that we are *wonderfully* and **fearfully** made (Psalms 139:14).

If this information written in 2003 about Good Medicine does not make one want to begin a prayer life, create a prayer life, or build upon a prayer life that we already have, then I don't know what would move us to prayer other than a life threatening illness. This information was given over eight years ago, and we have rapidly advanced in spiritual, scientific, and medical fields. The prophets of today are telling us

God is escalating time. This is revealed by a greater focus on the healing and prayer movements.

We are truly closing the gap between heaven and earth as a result of our revelation of who Christ is. *His* will is being done on earth as it is in Heaven (the Lord's Prayer). "For such a time as this," we are Disciples of Christ and mandated to help bring Heaven to Earth. **Prayer and divine healing are the Children's bread**. We are to follow Jesus' example as the Bible instructed us to do. What example did Christ give?

Divine Healing

Jesus is just as concerned about our physical healing as he is about our emotional and spiritual healing. Our state of being — spirit, soul, and body — is of the upmost concern of our Savior. This is obvious by the emphasis Jesus put on healing.

And to prove my point, Holman Illustrated Bible Dictionary says that **one-fifth** of the gospels (Matthew, Mark, Luke and John) report Jesus' miracles. Sounds like good healing press to me. Fourteen physical and mental healings are also recorded in the Bible. No doubt God wants us to have a healthy body and sound mind. I was surprised to read that Holman also stated the word **"psychosomatic"** means **"soul**

and body". III John 2 speaks of John wishing his friend, Galus, to be healthy and that his "soul prosper". Health is revealed in our bodies and our "prosperous soul" (mind, will, intellect, and emotion), and is manifest in our character and actions.

Forbid Them Not

In Jesus' time, there were multitudes of physical manifestations of sickness and emotional dysfunctions. These emotional problems were dealt with in various deliverance methods — not only by Jesus, but also by his trained disciples (Matthew 9 & 10). Even one of Jesus' followers questioned others that were ministering healing. The disciples said these others were laying hands on the sick. Jesus said, in essence, don't worry about them. **"Forbid them not; for he that is not against us is for us"** (All things work for his good). Check these scriptures out - Luke 9:50 and Mark 9:40.

This is definitely something to **selah** – stop and think about. If Christ is being lifted up by someone and we don't know or understand their motives, then if they're not against him, let's assume they are for him. Christ says, **"If I be lifted up I'll draw all men unto me."** Sounds like a covenant promise to me.

Christ used numerous methods to heal. He laid hands on the person; He used clay, spit, or whatever was available at the moment. He prayed, forgave sins, declared healing, gave commands, anointed with oil, and used the afflicted person's faith and the faith of their loved ones to heal. My thought is His healing techniques were unlimited, but not all were written.

And I don't believe this is the whole story. I envision Christ doing unimaginable healings. His love and compassion was a **supernatural** emotion that was greater than the sum of His physical being.

So if Jesus prayer and healing of all kinds (let's not put God in our box) is not *Good Medicine,* then I don't know what is. This is the medicine I use, and it has kept me healthy.

When we truly realize what *Good Medicine* is, prayer (just talking to God), that affects our whole being, then we have moved into a new dimension of *faith*. Meaning, you have gone to a new faith level where the anointing of prayer **breaks the yokes of bondage** over your physical, mental, emotional, and spiritual being.

Let us now activate our faith and belief system by the following.

Good Medicine Declarations

- *I declare I am wonderfully and fearfully made*
- *I declare God's healing provision is my bread*
- *I declare prayer, the Good Medicine of God, is my life force*
- *I declare the God Particle has been found and is in me*
- *I declare I have a healthy body, a sound mind, and Christ's love regulates my emotions*
- *I declare Divine Health is my bread of life*

Your Prayer of Good Medicine
Adapted from Psalm 91

Lord God, thank you for providing a secret place for me under the shadow of your wings.

You are my refuge and fortress, and in You I will trust.

Lord, my trust in You will deliver me from my enemies and snares that are out to entrap me.

You said You would cover me with Your wings, and Your truth will be my shield and buckler.

You are my truth. Your truth is my battle provisions against all the fiery darts of the enemy.

Fear will not grip me in the night season nor in the day time. No evil arrows will pierce me.

Because of Your shield of protection, and Your extended right hand, thousands will not be allowed to attack me, and evil will not be able to attach itself to me.

With my eyes, You have allowed me to see the reward of the wicked because:

You are my Lord

You are my refuge

You are the most high

You are my habitation

I love You and bless You, Lord, for giving Your angels charge over me to keep me in all my ways.

You truly are Jehovah Jireh, my God who provides. You provided Christ so I could rule and rein with You.

Amen and Amen

Who Declares
The Glory of the Lord?

*God's word declares His glory and
man walks it out.*
— Anita Mason 02/25/12

It is the Heavens that declare the glory of the Lord, and the skies proclaim His handiwork (Psalms 19:1). Were *you* aware of that? And this is not all that Psalms 19 reveals to us. *It gives us a depth of spiritual insight that God reveals to us about Himself*.

Do you ever just sit and wonder about whom God is and why He made man in His image? Does He look like man or is man an image of what He would want to look like? I'm impressed that He would want to look like us or us to look like Him.

Remember in Psalms 139:14 His word says we are fearfully and wonderfully made. Would it interest you to know that *the word Wonderful is a title of the Messiah* (Isaiah 9:6)? Another confirmation is we are wonderfully made in His image. God had to think what He created was fantastic, beginning with Adam and Eve who were also created in His own image, His own likeness. (Genesis 1)

The God Team

He also had a team He worked with to bring forth our creation. God said, "Let us make man in our image, in our likeness." What a team—*Father, Son (Jesus), and Holy Spirit—that hoovers over all creation and continues to do so.*

I love the thought and promise from the Father that the Holy Spirit is with me, in me, and all around me. Just thinking about this, I feel the love and comfort of the Holy Spirit. However, God is a God of order, and He makes all things perfect in His time. He will perfect us (meaning teach, instruct) if we are yielded to Him and meet His provisions.

The Bible, when read, will reveal all God's promises, provisions, and even His consequences of an unyielded, sin-filled life. That is *our part—to read, study, and know His word in order to know His presence and promises.* Let's move on. I have more to share about Psalm 19 that is pressing on my heart.

Works of His Hand

When I was meditating on how the heavens declare His glory and the skies reveal the works of His hands, the next verse caught my breath. *Day after day, they continue to speak of His glory, and night after night, His knowledge is manifest.* (Psalm 19:2) Imagine this, our days, every day, speaks *God's language* to us through His *creation*. And night after night, knowledge is continually released on our behalf. This includes dreams in the night season. I will be sharing more about dreams in another chapter.

Voice of Creation

Psalm 19:1 states the heavens declare the glory of God. And Psalm 19:3 declares there is no sound, there is no speech, no words are spoken, *yet a voice* (of some fashion) *is released through all the earth.* What is being said is a sound that goes out into all the earth, and *"their words to the ends of the world."*

Can you grasp the depths of what the Father is telling us about Himself? Well, with faith in God and His word, you can believe what Hebrews 11:1 says. "Faith is the substance of things hoped for and the evidence of things not seen." ***Faith*** is a ***substance,*** and His word is going from one circuit of the earth to the other; this is the evidence of something we can't see but can know by observing the heavens and the environment.

I envision this awesome information as, there is not a day or a night that God's spirit is not sending us messages that reveal His glory. ***The Holy Spirit hovering over all creation from beginning to end does not have to make a sound or speak to be heard.*** Creation itself has a voice. This supernatural, unspoken voice is all over the earth, and His spiritual words will be with us to the end of the world.

God's Cocoon

If you can grab hold of this, you will realize we are constantly cocooned in a spiritual atmosphere that God has created for us. God has made every provision (most unknown by man) for us to have a spiritual life and have it abundantly. God will continue to release what we need through the day and bring forth that knowledge in the night season. I remind you—the ***spirit has a voice of its own. The Spirit speaks to us with sounds, and without sounds; basically, a spirit language of its own.***

What am I really expressing to you? The presence of the Lord is always surrounding us. His manifest presence is always with us. This is the unseen world that the Bible speaks of that we know very little about. I don't know about you, but I'm intending to find out more about the Father's unseen word.

Can we hear, know, or feel His presence *that is always with us*? It is not a feeling. *It's a knowing. His Word says He will never leave us or forsake us.* This is only a portion of our knowing.

His word states:

> *God is not a man that he should lie.*
> *Nor a son of man that he should repent.*
> *Has He said, and will He not do?*
> *Or has He spoken, and will he not make it good? (Numbers 23:19)*

This scripture declares God's words to us. They will fulfill what He has spoken from one end of the earth to the other. You can take this to your heavenly bank account. It is eternal.

An All Knowing God

Another way of clarifying all the above is God is **all knowing, forever knowing, always present and forever present**. Just because we don't feel or sense His presence does not mean He is not with us. Often, it means *we are not* with Him.

He is the same always. We are the ones who change with every wind of doctrine which limits *our awareness* of His holy presence. Remember God's word, ***"He is not a man that He should lie..."*** This brings me to the last comment I want to make in Psalms. This reminds me — I have claimed verses seven to nine as my own on many occasions. Verse seven states, "the law of the Lord is perfect..." The rest of the verses declare His glory and what it does for us:

— **The law of the Lord is perfect, converting the soul; the testimony of the Lord is sure, making wise the simple;**

— **The statues of the Lord are right, rejoicing the heart; the commandment of the Lord is pure, enlightening the eyes;**

– **The fear of the Lord is clean enduring forever; the judgments of the Lord are true and righteous altogether.**

Let your heart be open and meditate on what *He says* and what *He does* pertaining to the above scriptures. He:

Converts the soul

Makes wise the simple

Rejoices the heart

Enlightens the eyes

The fear of the Lord endures forever

All these spiritual provisions are ours to embrace

Scripture adds in Psalm 19 that He has true and righteous judgments. All of this is more to be desired for than much fine gold, sweeter than honey and the honeycomb. We are warned if we keep all the above we are in for a Great Reward. Do we do these things for a reward? Heavens no! *We do this to declare the glory of the Lord.*

Agree With Me In Prayer

Lord, the heavens and the firmament declare your glory. It is in my prayer that I declare your glory. Father, give to me your depth of spiritual revelation on the Heavens, the atmosphere, and the earth that your spirit hoovers over. I want to have a new knowing of You and how the Holy Spirit encapsules us on Your behalf.

I choose to hear Your sounds that the natural man cannot hear. I call forth Your words that go from one end of the earth to the other to minister to me. Father, I do not pretend to know or understand Your unseen world. However, my prayer is to enter Your dimension of heavenly places and see how, from Your Word, we could sit in heavenly places with You now. I am in agreement with Your Word and will declare the glory to You Lord.

Amen in Agreement

Declarations
From Psalm 19

- *I declare the glory of the Lord will be upon me and around me*

- *I declare the Holy Spirit hovers over me for I am God's creation*

- *I declare God made all things perfect in His time and I am in His time*

- *I declare the law of the Lord is perfect converting my soul*

- *I declare my Lord will cleanse me from secret faults and keep me from presumptuous sins*

- *I declare the words of my mouth and the meditations of my heart will be acceptable in His sight*

Do You Want God To Touch You?

His Word confirms that He Has already touched you

Praise Be to God in all His Glory. He touched man. He touched me.

Psalms 139:13 – *Lord You have formed my inward parts; You covered me in my mother's womb. I will praise You for I am fearfully and wonderfully made.*

Psalms 139:17 – *How precious also are Your thoughts to me, O God! How great is the sum of them! If I should count them, they would be more in number than the sand; When I awake I am still with You.*

Psalms 40:15 – *Many, O Lord, My God are Your wonderful works which You have done, and Your thoughts toward me be recounted to you in order; If I could declare and speak of them, they are more than can be numbered.*

He touched man:

Genesis 1:26 *– Then God said, "Let Us make man in Our image, according to Our likeness; let them have dominion over the fish of the sea, over the birds of the air, and over the cattle, over all the earth and over every creeping thing that creeps on the earth."*

Psalms 8:4 *– What is man that You are mindful of him, and the son of man that You visit him? For You have made me a little lower than the angels and You have crowned me with glory and honor.*

Psalms 8:6 *– You have made him to have dominion over the works of Your hands. You have put all things under His feet.*

Also He touched:

Psalms 8:7 *– The birds of the air, and the fish of the sea that pass through the paths of the sea.*

Psalms 9 *– O' Lord, My Lord. How excellent is Your name in all the earth.*

We declare again Praise be to God in all His glory. He touched man – **__He touched me.__**

Selah – pause and think about God's touch.

Ho! Everyone Who Thirsts

When you have had all you can hold
to drink and you're still thirsty, try the
water of life, it never runs dry.

– Anita Mason 3-1-12

A re you thirsty? Are you dry? Have you been so entangled in the cares of the world that you feel like a prune, all dried up and no moisture in your whole being?

Do you spend money foolishly or do you wish you had money to spend foolishly? In your work-place, are you satisfied with your wages?

The invitation is open to all. Isaiah 55:1 boldly states, *"Ho! Everyone who thirsts, come to the waters."* What are these waters? *"They are waters of life – a never ending stream of the Holy Spirit running through you that never runs dry"*. Are we really hearing what the Spirit is saying to us through these passages of scripture? Do we have listening ears? There is much I could say about hearing and *listening*; however, for the time being, I will briefly comment.

Listening is just as active as speaking. Active listening involves giving my full attention to someone in a non-judgmental way. It involves focusing *only* on the person who is speaking to me in verbal and non-verbal language. When this is applied, we have listening ears. *To hear* is not just hearing words, but receiving in fullness what a person *means and feels*. With good listening and hearing skills, we can receive what Jesus is sharing with us about His eternal water.

Imagine this...the water (messages, words, promises, and provisions) that Jesus gives us in the Epistle's is His eternal water. When we drink deeply from His wells, we will be that fountain of everlasting life. We need deeper revelation of his metaphorical messages. Let's launch our own containers (thoughts, words, deeds behaviors, study, and passion for Him) and draw deep into Christ's living word.

John 4 speaks of natural water (from the earth) and spiritual water that is Jesus himself. In this chapter, Jesus sat down by Jacob's well, and a Samaria woman came to draw water, and He said to her, *"Give me a drink."* After a short interchange of words, Jesus tells her, *"Whoever drinks of this water will thirst again but whoever drinks of the water that I shall give him will never thirst. But the water that I give him will become in him a fountain of water springing up into everlasting life.*"

The Lord Speaks

Isaiah 55 continues (I see the Lord whispering loud and passionately), *Listen carefully to me. "Incline your ear and come to Me. Hear* and your soul shall live;" He is telling us not only to *listen,* but also to *hear.* We listen to many noises that are around us and what is also being said by them. However, we do not always *hear* what one is saying and get the full concept of the message. "*Hear and your soul shall live*; what does He mean by our soul? Our soul consists of mind, will, intellect, and emotions. *He wants us to hear with our whole being.*

In this chapter, The Lord is getting ready to share with us an eternal promise that will keep the "*waters*" of life flowing through us continually— His everlasting covenant with us. *Listen* and *Hear* for the Lord states, "And I will make an everlasting covenant with You—the sure mercies of David." In Isaiah 55:4, the Lord states about David, "*Indeed,*

I have given him as a witness to the people." I might add, just read the Psalms, and you will know the depth of David's passion and testimony to the people and the fulfillment of his everlasting covenant with his Lord.

Isaiah 55:6 declares, "*Seek the Lord while He may be found, call upon Him while he is near.*" God's word is full of stories where God found man and man found God. *They knew when He was near, and everlasting covenants were formed.*

Do you know when He is near? *Listen* and you will *hear* Him *calling* your name softly, waiting for you to call upon Him while "*He is near*". It is the Lord's desire to make an everlasting covenant with you. With His covenant, you will never thirst again; His water never runs dry.

Covenant Prayer

Lord, I want an everlasting covenant with You. I choose your waters of life, that never ending stream of the Holy Spirit that never runs dry. Jesus assures me the water that He gives me will be a fountain of water springing up into everlasting life. I choose this everlasting life and ask Jesus to forgive my sins and trespasses. Be the Lord of my life as I receive Christ into my heart, and I accept Your everlasting covenant.

In Jesus Name Amen

A *confirming* word that David shares with us in Psalm 32:5 — "I acknowledge my sin to You and my iniquity I have not hidden." I said, "I will confess my transgressions to the Lord and You will forgive the inequity of my sin." This is why David is considered a man after God's own heart.

Selah

Water of Life

I Declare:

- **My thirst will be quenched, will be satisfied and fulfilled.**
- **I have a never ending stream of the Holy Spirit running through me that never runs dry**
- **I will listen carefully and incline my ears to hear from my Lord**
- **I will seek the Lord while He may be found and call upon Him while He is near**
- **With His everlasting covenant I will never thirst again**

Sign your name_____

Check out the awesome poem.

Awesome

I hear You in the silence.
I hear You in the storm.
I hear You in the baby's cry.
I see You in the dawn.

I feel Your peace each morning
And all throughout the day.
I feel Your peace at bedtime
And every time I pray.

Your awesomeness surrounds me
In everything I do.
How blessed I am to have a God
As wonderful as You.

-Frances Gregory Pasch

Out of the Darkness Into the Light?

Behold, the Lord's hand is not so
short that it cannot save; Nor is His
ear so dull that it cannot hear.

Isaiah 59:1

I always ask the Lord for a word pertaining to the upcoming year. I usually do this around New Year's Eve.

God is faithful. He always gives me something that I can cling to and build on for the rest of the year (not to mention to pass on to others). A portion will usually include a word about our nation. For instance, one of the words given to me the first of 2011 was, *"God's time vs. man's time. There are dimensions of time that God created for us that He will be revealing to us. And Israel is God's time table for the nation. Another word is pay close attention to what happens in Israel, this is not new, just a reminder.*" These are just *two* of the first of the year insights He gave me for our nation and for me.

For now, what can I say that has not already been said about the state of affairs our nation is in? My spirit is in a perpetual state of grief concerning what is happening nationally and internationally.

I don't want to be presumptuous, but it appears that our nation, which was founded on Christian principles, has been watered down to a country of *self-reliance,* not *God reliance*. It is my belief that we are in the *night season* of our spiritual life. There is much *spiritual darkness* all around us.

Today, as I am writing this, they just passed the Debt Crisis Bill. The Senate put a band-aid on our nation's money crisis. I have to admit I am not qualified to know and understand all about our economic blunders. We, as a nation, are in **spiritual darkness,** and if God does not somehow intervene, we will plunge into a depth of darkness that many may not recover (especially those that are not under His protective covering).

Take Note

Take note. I believe we are in *Spiritual Darkness* as a Nation. However, Christ spoke of a personal darkness. In Matthew 6:22 & 23, He says that the light in our body is the eye, and if our eye be single, in other words, focused with spiritual vision and discernment, then our whole body will be full of light. He adds, if our eye is evil, our whole body is full of darkness. In Luke 11:35, we are warned not to let the light that is in us be in darkness. I take that warning very seriously.

This brings to my remembrance the famous quote, *"The eyes are the windows to the soul."*

Our problem as a nation begins with us individually. And it begins with our soul. Our soul consists of *mind, will, intellect,* and *emotions*. We have a will that allows us choices and decisions concerning every aspect of our lives. This is where we make a decision to choose Christ who is our light, our candle, our illumination. Christ sent the Comforter, the Holy Spirit, to keep our spiritual and natural eyes enlightened and out of darkness. We must get a revelation of any spiritual darkness that we have been walking in. As long as we stay *comfortable* where we are, the enemy will continue to keep us in darkness. It is often said that if you're not moving forward, you're slipping backward. There is no such thing as no movement.

Are You Comfortable?

What does being *comfortable* in any type of darkness mean? This could possibly mean we can learn to be *comfortable* in any type of situation or relationship, good or bad, abusive or loving. When we are comfortable in any of these states (I am not saying this is what we necessarily want), we just don't always know the difference between good or bad situations we are living in. We live and personally structure our lives in what we're used to. Research calls this conditioning. In other words, we are *conditioned* to do what we do. The American Heritage Dictionary defines conditioned as *"prepared for a specific action, exhibiting or trained to exhibit, a new or modified response."*

Satan has modified, or in other words, changed, and deceived us into a watered down, weak, and powerless form of Christianity. Our nation is in state of financial crisis; we feel we are powerless as Christians to do anything about this. Since our whole nation is in an upheaval, we feel and sense the effects of this from the top (nation) to the bottom (individual). This is often defined as the *"Trickle down"* effect, meaning from international to the individual, we will *all* experience some degree of *aftershock*. In other words, no matter what happens, we will experience something from the impact from the top down.

Look Around

Just look around at all the crisis situations that have surrounded us—drought, flooding, fires, hurricanes, tsunamis, terrorism, etc. We are so focused on the "*cares of the world*" that we cannot keep our eye single, meaning focused, with spiritual discernment. Thus, as a nation and individually, we are fighting a tough battle with enemy forces all around us. Does this mean we are defeated? That our enemies will keep us in captivity to *spiritual darkness*? Heavens no!

Spiritual darkness fades when we make the choice to choose Christ and begin an understanding of the light that I'm sharing about; then we have moved into another realm of life that is what I call the *Supernatural*. The moment I chose Christ as my personal savior, I began a *Supernatural Journey*. One is not always aware of this concept of the spiritual realm that they have moved into. It would be my passion that Christians would get the revelation of *who they really are in Christ. How they walk in His light even when they are not aware of it*. This is not a feeling; it is a truth. Does this happen automatically? Yes, if you are truly abiding in Him. No, if this is just an intellectual assent. When we operate out of *intellect* instead of our *spirit,* the enemy of our souls will do whatever he possibly can to keep our spiritual and natural eyes blinded to the miraculous powers of God that have been imparted within us.

Our enemy has also deceived us to the point where we are comfortable in a state of spiritual darkness. I have observed that most of us have not received our intended promises from God. As a result, we are not receiving what Christ has already released – *the supernatural genetic DNA that is imbedded with us*.

We're hearing a lot about the miraculous and how God is pouring out *His Spirit* on all mankind. We are waiting on *miracles*, *signs,* and *wonders*. Well, we are a *miracle*, *sign,* and *wonder*. What we as a body of Christ are waiting on has already been released. We keep asking for something that *we already have. Christ is waiting on us to get the revelation of who we really are in Him and that we are supernatural just because He is.*

It does appear that the enemy of our souls has done whatever he possibly could to keep our spiritual eyes blinded to the *miraculous powers of God that have been imparted within us*. Satan, Lucifer the devil, even the Strong man or whatever he is called, has deceived us long enough. Would you call centuries of darkness long enough?

He has also deceived us to the point that we are comfortable in this state of spiritual darkness, and we have not received our intended promises from God. Let's choose not to be comfortable in any state of darkness.

Hear My Prayer O'Lord

Lord, I see that You are not pleased when we are in spiritual darkness. Therefore, Your arm that is not shortened will bring enlightment and healing to all. You shall sustain us by teaching us to put on your righteousness as a breastplate, and on our head, a helmet for salvation. Father, we also receive the breastplate of righteousness, and rejoice in Your healing power. Now, Lord Jesus, let us walk in peace and allow You to make all our crooked places straight.

Amen - My Protector

Declarations to Bring Forth Light

- I declare God will continually make provisions for us to walk in His light. These declarations are His provisions.
- I declare the Lord will bring me out of darkness into His marvelous light.
- I declare spiritual darkness will not invade my life.
- I declare the negative conditioning in my life will be revealed and healed.
- I declare I will receive every provision You will have made for me to have a victorious Christian life.
- I declare my spiritual eyes will no longer be darkened to God's spiritual enlightment.

Give Thanks to the Lord

Ignorance is Not Bliss

"Search me O God and know my heart, Try me and know my thoughts"
(Psalm 139)

Early one morning (in fact on August 31, 2011), I was in a searching mood. So I began to leaf through the pages of the New Testament in my bible (I use both NKJ and KJ bibles and others when needed). I remembered the familiar saying that the book of **Romans is the road to salvation**. This also reminded me of another familiar saying that I heard my mother quote through my entire early development (especially when she was making a point), "**Ignorance is not bliss.**" I'm thinking this is a great title for what is in my heart to share.

When my mother was correcting me and my sisters, and she thought we were not paying attention, she would make the statement "*ignorance is not bliss.*" For example, we had certain chores that were required of us. One of them was ironing our own clothes. When we slopped through the ironing process, she would use this term. "*Ignorance*" to us was "*who cares,*" just get it done.

On other occasions, I remember my mother saying "*Ignorance is Bliss.*" However, this was spoken when mother was joking with her friends or to herself. That saying was not reserved just for us. It takes half a lifetime to realize that mother was usually right. I especially feel that "*ignorance is not bliss*" when desiring to grow up spiritually.

The Word is NearYou

My attention is now parked on Romans chapter ten. One of my favorite scriptures is in this chapter. "*The word is near you, in your mouth and in your heart.*" This begins to resonate in me when, in the third verse, Paul admonishes Israel for being *ignorant* of God's word and establishing their own righteousness. Also, in Ephesians 4:18, Paul is speaking about the Gentiles understanding being darkened and separated from God through ignorance.

Now, I'm feeling compelled to pray for any ignorance that established me in my own self righteousness. I ask the Lord to wash me, cleanse me, and purify me from my own self righteousness and again submit myself to the righteousness of God. Now, I take a big breath and feel refreshed.

I continue reading, and I find this chapter in Romans will help keep me out of ignorance. After reading these verses, I am now feeling full. This same chapter tells us that Paul bears witness that the people have zeal for God, but not according to knowledge. I remember my own zeal and how my lack of knowledge often looked foolish as my zeal ran ahead of me. Paul tells us how ignorant many people are of God's righteousness. He states Moses writes about righteousness which is the *law,* but the scriptures say, "Christ is the end of the law for righteousness to everyone who believes" (Romans four).

Does this mean no more righteousness is required? Lord, no; it just means that **under the Law of Moses,** righteousness is not the same requirement for New Testament believers. Christ clarifies our righteousness.

The word says in Romans ten that if **"we say in our heart,"** we will ascend into heaven to find Christ; if we do not find Him there, then we will descend into the abyss and bring Christ "from the dead." The word says in verse six not to say these things in our heart (remember the heart can be deceitful above all things). Here is a great revelation in verse eight. "The word (meaning Christ who was made flesh to dwell among us, John 1:14) *is near you in your mouth and in your heart."*

Deuteronomy 30:14 (Old Testament) is the foundation for this New Testament revelation and states, **"But the word is very near you, in your mouth and in your heart, that you may do it."** I love this – the word is in *my mouth* that *I may do it*. We have authority; we have permission from the word of Christ that His word is in our heart, and we **can do it.** We can do what His word says we can do. We do not have to ascend or descend anywhere to find Christ. He is right here with us. He lives in our circumcised heart.

A Circumcised Heart

What is a *circumcised heart*? In the Old Testament, God required literal circumcision (Genesis 17: 9-10). This was under the law of the Abramic Covenant. In Abraham's Covenant, God required that the flesh of the foreskin of every man child be circumcised as a token of covenant between man and God.

In the New Testament, let's further examine what the word says about circumcision. In Romans two (check these scriptures out), beginning at verse 25, much is stated about circumcision. In verse 29, we are told one is a Jew who is inwardly circumcised in the heart, in the spirit, and not in the letter of the law. What does this mean to me? Well, let's read on.

In the next chapter, Romans 29:3 speaks of the heart. Verse 29 says, "Is He the God of the Jews only? Is He not also of the Gentiles? Yes, of the Gentiles also." Even in the Old Testament God stated "...**therefore, circumcise the foreskin of your heart and be stiff necked no longer**." What is this speaking to us about our God? He is more interested in the condition of our heart than keeping rigid laws.

The Holy Spirit is the one doing spiritual surgery on our hearts, without a knife and without man's hand, only the hand of God. Now one can understand how He lives in our circumcised hearts. By the way, our doctors do the physical surgery God does the spiritual surgery.

Grab hold of this spiritual revelation; we do not have to run to and fro, up or down, in or out, to find Christ. To find Christ, Romans 10:9 says, "Confess with your mouth the Lord Jesus Christ and believe in your heart that God has raised Him from the dead." We believe with our heart and confess with our mouth, and whoever calls on Him will be saved. This assures us of Christ's *instant* life in us. Instant to me means it is sealed in the *now*.

Walking Epistles

I love this special word in Romans ten. God's sound has gone out into all the earth, and His words to the end of the world. How? By the feet of those who preach the gospel of peace, those who bring good news. Those who love Christ and *activate* their belief are those "**Walking Epistles Read of all Men**" and are the ones who bring the good news from one end of the earth to the other. I want to draw your attention back to John 1:14—this powerful word that Christ is *near you in your mouth and in your heart.* Let's not be ignorant in understanding the matters of the heart that God has revealed to us through His word.

There are three strategies that Satan will use to deceive our hearts and keep us from confessing God's truths. These strategies are ignorance, deception, disobedience.

<u>Ignorance</u> – Lack of knowledge can cause us to perish (Proverbs 29:18). God does not excuse ignorance. In fact, He tells us what to do to rid ourselves of it. "The book of law shall not depart out of thy mouth, but thou shalt meditate therein day and night to all that is within therein; for then thou shalt make

thy way prosperous and then thou shalt have good success" (Joshua 1:8).

Deception – Especially in our perceptions of His word. Incorrect doctrine which consists of misunderstanding and misapplication of Gods truth. Galaltians 6:7 says, "Do not be deceived, God is not mocked; for whatsoever a man sows, that he will also reap."

Disobedience – We will enjoy the blessings and benefits of God if we obey His commandments. Ephesians five states, "Let no one deceive you with empty words, for because of these things the wrath of God comes upon the son's of disobedience." The good news is our obedience silences the enemy.

These three strategies are inconclusive to all that I could and probably should explain. Plus, I could talk endlessly about them, but that is not my focus. My purpose is to bring some thought provoking ideas that will prevent the enemy from defeating us.

Our Enemy

Speaking of the enemy, he will stop at nothing to do whatever he can to defeat us. This brings to mind something I heard a long time ago. (I do not recall where I heard it). God allows us to be tested through one: *the applause of men* and two: *the pressures of life*. It doesn't take a "rocket scientist" to understand how the enemy uses men's applause to keep us in arrogance, self centeredness, and self-elevation. Also, the enemy uses the pressures of life to keep us uptight, fearful of the future, full of anxiety and stress that eventually causes physical illness or possibly premature death. So, let us be aware that the *applause of man* and the *pressures of life* do not have to defeat us.

The Holy Spirit will guide us into all truth about ourselves when our focus is on Him. He will raise us above the pressures of life and applause of men by the spirit of truth that He imparts within us. The spirit of truth will expose Satan's strategies of *ignorance*, *deception*, and *disobedience*.

We will be strengthened by allowing the Holy Spirit to walk through all the trails of life with us. My ending personal thought is, grow up spiritually and do not be ignorant of God's Word. *Remember Ignorance is not Bliss.*

Prayer

Lord, You have proved my heart; You are welcome to visit me in all the seasons of my life. You have tried me; therefore, I'm asking You to give me an understanding heart to be able to discern between good and evil. Tactics of the enemy will not entrap me. Create in me a clean heart, O God, and renew a right spirit with me. And Your peace, God, which passes all understanding, will keep my heart and mind through Jesus Christ.

Yours Truly

Declarations to Search Out the Heart

Here are suggested declarations to say out loud to allow the Lord to bring clarity to your heart:

*Lord, I **declare** not to be ignorant of the matters of my heart.*

*I **declare** I will not walk in ignorance of Your word.*

*I **declare** deception will not steal Your truth from me.*

*I **declare** I choose to walk in obedience of Your laws, precepts, and truths.*

*I **declare** I can do all things through Christ who strengthens me.*

Work these things out in me Lord and do it now!!

In Jesus' Name

It's All In The Timing

This day God, You have made it, you have appointed it, You have blessed it, you have anointed it.

— Anita Mason 1979

" **J**esus said to them, My time has not yet come, *but your time is always ready*." John 7:6

One of my favorite sayings is, "*we must get a deeper understanding of time.*" God created time for the natural man, and we have locked ourselves into man's earthly time. One of my revelations is God is not locked into our time (but we live our lives as though He is), and it is my passion to move out of man's time into God's time.

Jeremiah 23:23 says, *"Am I a God near at hand"* *says the Lord, "and not a God afar off?"* God speaks to Jeremiah and states he is a *now* God. So when we meditate about God's time, we realize we are on earth, and he is heaven, and we have been brought forth to establish God's kingdom on earth.

God is not locked into our time. Scripture tell us that "Jesus Christ is the same *yesterday, today*, and *forever*" (Hebrews 13:8). Wow, grab hold of this! God is reminding us that He is timeless. He is in our *yesterday*, He is in *today,* and He is in the *future*.

Twice in Revelation it is made quite clear God is not locked into any time—"I am the Alpha and the Omega, the Beginning and the End." I am actually doing what Isaiah 41:21 tells us to do, *"Present your case says the Lord; bring forth your strong reasons."*

Present Your Case

I'm presenting my case, 2 Peter 3:8 says, "But beloved, do not forget this one thing, that with the Lord one day is a thousand years and a thousand years as one day." Psalms 90:4 also confirms, *"For a thousand years in Your sight are like yesterday when it is past, and like a watch in the night."* In II Timothy 4:2, we read *"Be ready in season and out of season."*

We need to get a profound revelation of what this scripture is declaring to us. As a result of these powerful words that God is speaking to us, our healing prayer can go into the pain and heartache of *yesterday* that has kept whom I'm praying with in captivity to the past. That person is often frozen or stuck in another time.

Since Jesus is the same in our yesterdays and tomorrows, I can take that hurting person to that place in time of wounding or pain because Christ goes right there in the midst of that situation to heal them.

When Christ sees us, He sees our beginning and our end – *all at once*. It is difficult for us to understand how this can happen because of the way we view time. God saw us when we were created in our mother's womb (Jeremiah 1:5), and all through our lifespan (all at once) until the time that we cease to exist on Earth and beyond. In other words, He sees our developmental time line from beginning to end in less than a split second. Any wounds, hurts, or traumas from the past can be healed as quick as the speed of light (186,000 miles per second).

Why would anyone want prayer back to when they were conceived in the womb? I can answer that concern. Because many conceptions are an accident or unwanted pregnancy. This results in rejection from one or both parents. Possibly there was violence or abuse. This impacts the emotional development of the unborn child.

Also, these situations definitely affect the spiritual part of us. This is called *"Failure to Thrive,"* where, after birth, the infant is listless and appears to have little zest for life. Meaning, the child's spirit is not matured enough to receive the gift of life. This often began in the womb. One example may be if the child is not wanted or there is not appropriate and loving care of self and baby during pregnancy. Also, if the child is not given enough nurturing from the parents, could result in a listless infant that (research has documented) may result in death.

Yesterday, Today and Forever

As a result, one of the ways I move in God's time (through prayer) is to minister to hurting people by going into the past to get to the root of their pain. I am still amazed at how God heals *yesterday*, *today*, and *forever* when we believe and understand that He is the creator of time. However, *He's not locked into time, especially not into my time*. My prayer is that this makes sense because God's time verses man's time is difficult to explain our spiritual healing.

As a licensed counselor, I am very careful to honor my clients, and the places that we go to in prayer must be their choice. It has been my privilege to pray with hundreds of hurting people and see them set free from past trauma. Past trauma, unhealed, distorts the whole concept of who they are and where they need to be advancing in their spiritual journey (Webster's Dictionary defines trauma as an *emotional shock with lasting psychic effects*).

Traumatized people develop distorted thoughts. Distorted thoughts work from the inside to the outside of us. Meaning, if we have emotionally distorted thoughts, eventually they will manifest in our physical being. Understanding this concept is a delicate process. That is why, when working with a person in trauma, the ultimate healing must be in God's time. He has given me the discernment to know His timing and not to move too quickly. This could abort what He is doing in the presence of healing.

His Fire of Love Ignited

Isaiah 42:3 reveals to us what a loving, caring Father we have: "*A bruised reed He will not break, and smoking flax He will not quench*. He will not bruise, break, or put out what little bit of light or fire we may still have within us – wherever there is a flicker, *His fire of love can be ignited*."

The above promise in Isaiah helps me to be cautious with His loved ones—especially when I'm working with traumatized people.

I believe I am in God's time to be in this type of ministry and counseling. I see many miraculous healings that are set in *His time*.

Jesus said His time had not yet come, but *your time* is *always ready*.

One might ask, "Always ready for what?" Isn't He telling us that our time is God's time and that He has imparted into each of us a readiness of faith, a belief that if we would tap into the depth of the Holy Spirit that was provided us, our time to be "*always ready*" ("instant in season and out of season") *is now*.

Another way I interpret this is I believe Christ is telling us that there is a place in Him where we can always be ready for everything He has called us to do, and it will be His time, not ours. My prayer is that you will have a depth of understanding of another time outside of our time that is God's *eternal* time. At certain times and seasons, I believe we can enter into His time.

Some have called this time and season Portals just like Jacob called his encounter "the gate of heaven." God sent His angels to ascend and descend on the ladder that was set up on earth (Genesis 28:12).

Christ said we could sit in Heavenly Places with Him. *Let's ascend and descend with Him, shifting our time to His Time*.

A prayer to seek God in His time

Lord, give me a revelation of *Your time*. You said in Your Word that *You* are a rewarder of those that diligently seek *You*. Well, I am seeking You in the *here and now* to know what Your timing is in my life. My time is in Your hands, and I choose to move in Your time and season. Provide me the same ladder You provided Jacob in his dream, the same ladder that brought an open heaven with Angelic visitation. Open my spiritual eyes to see and let me sit in those Heavenly places that You have already provided for me for I am a diligent seeker.

In Jesus' Name - Amen

Declarations that Determine Time

- *I declare and acknowledge that Your time is always ready.*
- *I declare that Christ is revealing to me, He is the same yesterday, today, and forever because He is in all time.*
- *I declare I will present my case for all my concerns to my Heavenly Father.*
- *I declare I will let the Holy Spirit teach me how to be mature, be strong, and be consistent in all seasons.*
- *I declare I will allow You, Lord, to teach me how to diligently seek You.*
- *I declare the areas where I have been hurt or bruised; my loving Father will not break or quench my spirit. And His love for me will stay ignited through all my healing processes.*
- *I declare I am in God's time, and my time is now.*

Last but not least, I declare that Christ has provided a place in Him where I will always be ready for anything.

In His Time - Amen

The Comforter

A real healing occurs when you do the right thing in the worst of circumstances.

– Anita Mason 05/09/2000

I n the Book of John, Jesus describes the Holy Spirit as the **Comforter**. He tells His disciples that the **Comforter** will not come (as His replacement) until He leaves. Jesus continually prepares His disciples for His absence from them to be with the Father.

I found it interesting that in John 16:5 Jesus tells His disciples that He is going back to "**Him that sent Me,**" and He appears to marvel at the fact that they do not ask Him **where He's going**. They are sorrowful, and their hearts are filled with sadness, but they still do not ask.

However, there is still no follow up questions from His disciples to ask where He is going. This appears to be part of our human nature. We want to know, but we **fear what we may find out**. What were the disciples afraid to know and find out about their Savior? They could have asked Him. Why didn't they inquire (at this time) about where He was going and why?

Another reason apart from fear could be that our insecurities about ourselves, and life, intimidate us to not ask these important (in this case needful) questions about the future. The unanswered questions of the disciples had to be a concern on Christ's mind because He mentioned this matter again in John 16:17. What is this that He says to us: "A little while and you will not see Me, and again a little while, and you will see Me and, because I go to the Father?"

He knew that His disciples were inquiring among themselves about what He was telling them. By this time, Jesus knew they were bursting at the seams to ask Him about the things He was telling them. "**You see Me now, in a little while you won't see Me because I go to the Father**."

The Mind Reader

By the way, what they did not realize was that Jesus knew their every thought and could **read their minds**. He knew they desired to ask questions. Just like them, we desire to ask Jesus questions. He knows what we are thinking. In fact, ***He knows our thoughts before we think them***. He wants us to inquire of Him the things we desire to know. Even the thoughts we dare not to express out loud, He knows because **He reads the heart**. What we put in our hearts is what is going to come out of our mouths. Even if we are not speaking thoughts out loud, messages are rolling around in our heads, either building up or tearing down our whole being. Our thoughts find their way into the very core of our being. Jesus wants us to express what we are questioning Him about to bring our thoughts out into the open. Why? Because this open expression of our thoughts are for us – not for Him. He wants **us** to know what is in our hearts. When we express what we are thinking (out loud), then we uncover answers that will help cleanse our hearts. Acknowledging what needs to be cleansed is the first step in healing.

Another scriptural way to bring our thoughts out into the open is the joy of the Lord.

Fruitful Joy

In John 16, Jesus explains what the disciples sorrow will be like when He's gone and that when he sees them again, their hearts will rejoice; and the biggie here is "**and your joy no one will take from you**" (Verse 22). **Joy is a fruit of the spirit**. It is not an emotion that man can conjure up. When reading the stories of all the disciples, the one thing they never lost was the joy of the Lord.

They went through trials, tribulations, heartaches, and pain but never lost joy. Of all the fruits of the spirit, with the exception of love, joy must be one of the most powerful attributes of Christ that He left for the **Comforter** to fulfill in us. The **Comforter**, who is the **Comforter**? He is the helper (V7). **He is the convictor of sin, righteousness, and judgment** (V8). **He is the spirit of truth; He tells of things to come** (V13). Most importantly, Jesus said, "**He will take of what is mine and declare it to you**" (V15). **Wow, another confirmation how important it is to declare a thing so it is established** (Job 22:8).

Just remember, whatever we declare must already be established by the Word of the Lord. Job 22:22 reads, "**And lay up His words in your heart**." When His words are written in our hearts, we can declare that word because it's in the heart of God. He has released that word to us to declare it and bring it forth from the unseen world to the seen world.

All God's words are in the unseen (non physical) world just waiting for us to establish them in our hearts and in our world. I think this is about as deep as I need to go on this subject for now. It is difficult for me to explain what is truly in my heart about the Holy Spirit, the **Comforter**.

How can one adequately describe the inner workings of the heart when the Holy Spirit has written things that are indescribable on it? I could write endlessly about what Christ said and revealed in the book of John. What an awesome revelatory book. **The book of John is one of the most exciting, mysterious, secretive, metaphoric, convicting, confirming, demanding,** and **loving** books of the Bible. Do I have an agreement on this?

John is about God's last message to man. God's last and final word through Jesus brought the **Comforter** to us. I urge you to read the whole book of John and let the Holy Spirit comfort you. No matter what is going on in your life or what you're going through, God is with you.

His word says, "I will never leave you or forsake you." **He may not jerk us up out of our circumstances; however, He will walk through all of them with us.** This is what the **Comforter** is all about. This is the **promise** and **provision** Christ left with us.

A Love Letter to the Holy Spirit

Dear Holy Spirit,

I love the warmth of Your love, the comfort of Your love. You are my life, the breath in my nostrils, the cells of my being. I have no purpose in life except to follow You into truth, love, and perfection through Christ. You are my very thoughts, my meditations, my prayer, the altar of my being as I join as one with You. I must have and know Your presence, lest I die. My life is a vapor without Your coverings and protection. Holy Spirit, teach me how to live as one with You.

Love, Anita

_____ (your name here)

Comforting Declarations

- I **declare** I will allow the Comforter, the Holy Spirit, to invade my life and give me direction.
- I **declare** when I have questions for my Savior, I will speak them out. I will not lock hidden secrets in my heart from the Lord.
- I **declare** I will not be deceived into believing that Christ does not know my heart, mind, and thoughts. I **declare He knows all**.
- I **declare** joy will be fruitful in my life. and the joy of the Lord is truly my strength.

Seal these declarations Lord in Jesus' name.

Why God, Why?

Questioning God is man's way of questioning his own lifelong insecurities about eternity.

— *Anita Mason 12/19/11*

"God, why did you do this? Why did you allow this to happen?" Sound familiar? When we aren't asking ourselves these questions, we spend time assuming we know the answers to them. This is not good. Why is it not good to assume? Because the word says so – there is a sin of presumption. (Psalm 19:13)

Let's read on and not assume anything, but let God's word speak clearly to us. The word clearly and firmly says we often cause things to happen to ourselves. In the book of Jeremiah, the word of the Lord came to Jeremiah, stating how He formed Jeremiah in the womb and how He put words into Jeremiah's mouth and set him over Nations and

Kingdoms. Jeremiah's task was to **"root out, pull down, to destroy and throw down, to build and to plant." (Jeremiah 1:10)**

Why did God touch and speak to Jeremiah in such a fashion? Why was so great of an assignment on him? In verse 16, the Lord tells all: "I will utter My judgments against them concerning all their wickedness. Because they have forsaken Me, burned incense to other gods and worshipped the works of their own hands." Could **God speak any clearer?!**

Building a Case

God strengthens Jeremiah in Chapter 1 verse 18, and the case against the children of Israel continues in the subsequent scriptures:

Note, what the Lord says in the second chapter of Jeremiah verse 9, *"Therefore, I will yet bring charges against you."* Says the Lord, "And against your children's children I will bring charges." (Sounds like generational suffering to me!)

God continues to build His case in Chapter 2 verse 13, stating, **"For my people have committed two evils; they have forsaken me the fountain of living waters, and hewn themselves cisterns-broken**

cisterns that can hold no water." (Are our bellies empty of living water?)

Also, what does God mean by these "two evils?" God speaks to us through His word and our nature on how we have forsaken Him. Is God revealing to us that our **choices** which caused the judgments spoken to Jeremiah would happen to (us) like the children of Israel?

Here is my point. Beginning with your thoughts, to what comes out of our mouth, is what I might call "a lamp unto our feet and light unto out path." What light or illuminations (thoughts) are you allowing to guide your feet and light your path? "Our thoughts are released through the tongue. Out of the abundance of the heart the mouth speaks." Job 15:6 is one of the deepest spiritual insights that gives us revelation to God's word—**that our own thoughts and the words that come forth from our mouths condemn us**. Let this insight and revelation sink deeply into your spirit. Another example is expressed in Luke 19 where Jesus shares a parable about servants. The master is talking to one of His servants, sharing a very profound word with the servant. *"Out of your own mouth I will judge you, you wicked servant."* My thought is I do not want to be one that will be judged by my negative outbursts.

What Am I Eating?

Our greatest wisdom comes from Proverbs 13:2-3, *"A man shall eat well by the fruit of his mouth: but the soul of the unfaithful feeds on violence, He who guards his mouth preserves his life. But he who opens wide his lips shall have destruction."*

What are we eating by the fruit of our mouths? Could it be any clearer that we are responsible for what happens to us? Remember, our own mouths condemn us. The Lord makes it clear that He will judge us by *what comes out of our mouths*. Why? Because what we say comes from our thoughts.

Let's choose to grow up and put away childish mentality about the issues of life that God gets the blame. His word clearly states *we must take respon- sibility for our choices and what we say*. Thus, as a result of our own *choices, actions, and the words we speak, judgment is brought upon* **ourselves.** God is such a gracious and loving God. He would *not do to us what we do to ourselves*. He is a God of justice, righteousness, and judgment, and not a **condemning** God. Remember, *our own mouth condemns us! "Man has joy by the answer of his mouth"* (Proverbs 15:23). "The joy of the Lord is our strength" (Philippians 4:13). May joy be the fruit that comes forth from our mouths by the following prayer.

Pray to release condemnation and self judgment:

I return to you, O Lord, the God of my salvation. You are a merciful God who does not remain angry forever. Lord, I acknowledge my sin of self-condemnation. Lord, forgive me for judging and condemning others with my petty self righteousness. As an act of my will, I choose to break up my fallow ground, and I will not sow among thorns. I circumcise myself to You, Lord, and allow You to take away the foreskin of my heart just for You, my Beloved Lord. Now, Lord, I receive my promises You gave in Your word (Jeremiah 3:14) that when I return, You would give me shepherds according to Your heart who will feed me with knowledge and understanding. Your promises continue in verse 19. You shall call me "My Father" and not turn away from me. As I receive your promises, I call you "My Father," and I will not turn away from You.

It is me, Lord,
Your Loving Child

Declarations for Abundant Life:

- I **declare,** Lord, I will use wisely the choices You have given me.
- I **declare** You are my fountain of living water, and I will not go about my own way.
- I **declare** any bitterness in my heart will be found by You, Lord, and released.
- I **declare** You are a lamp unto my feet and a light unto my path.
- I **declare** joy will be the fruit that comes forth from my life

_____ (your name) Seals
these declarations

Stix and Stones

What I say today will impact all my tomorrows.

– Anita Mason 7/9/2000

I remember that, as a young school girl growing up, my sisters, Georgia and Elna, and I would call each other names when we got mad. We might say "you big baby," "you're mean," "I don't like you," "I hate you," and so on and so on. Children are notorious for name calling.

One point I want to make is that the name calling in my day was almost sanctified compared to the names that are used today to hurt and wound. We would chant back to each other **"Sticks and Stones may break my bones but names will never harm me."** What a deception, for most of us know and carry the scars that names have seared into our being (especially in childhood).

I have asked myself, "When did Satan deceive mankind to make us swallow and believe a lie that words would never harm us?" God answered and reminded me about the serpents lie and deception in the Garden of Eden—case closed.

Proverbs reminds us that words do both good and evil. **"Death and life are in the power of the tongue and those who love it will eat its fruit"** (Proverbs 18:21). Let's examine other scriptures pertaining to our tongue.

The word of God confirms there is little truth in the **Sticks and Stones** childhood jingle. Reality is that if we are attacked by **Sticks** and **Stones,** our body will heal. However, wounds caused by malicious, thoughtless words cut deep within us and, unless healed, will last our lifetime. Often these are our words we speak to ourselves.

On the other hand, uplifting words wisely spoken are life giving, comforting, and healing. In God's word, from beginning to end, He reveals to us the power of the spoken word. In turn, when we speak His word, we have been given the authority to heal and make whole.

Psalms 19:1-4 states, "The heavens and the firmament declare the Glory of God and show his handiwork; their line is gone out through all the Earth and their **words to the end of the world**." "Day unto day utters speech." Are you aware that our days are speaking something enlightening to us? **Lord, tune our ears in to hear daily what you are "uttering" to us.**

God's words are continually floating around from the beginning of time to the end of time. I believe that every word we speak has a circuit of its own and that the words we speak today will go to the end of eternity. **Romans 10:15 states that there is a sound that goes into all the Earth including words unto the end of the world**.

Wordiness

Wow, these are sobering thoughts. How about another one? Every word we speak, and also our thoughts, are manifested in our bodies. Words become imbedded into our flesh. All words are moving forces in our body. Scientific researchers tell us that our bodies continually vibrate.

Mankind is connected in such a way that our own vibrations affect not only our environment, but also those we have contact with. In summary, **if our words are moving forces, then it stands to reason that our cells have continuous vibration**.

The words that we speak to ourselves begin their own circuit through our bodies. When these words are released, they have the power of **self-fulfillment**. This is why it's important what we think about ourselves. Why? **"You are snared by the words of your mouth; you are taken by the words of your mouth." (Proverbs 6:2).** If we could receive this scriptural revelation of how our own words ensnare us, it would free us from self bondage.

My thoughts on word power remind me of an article in the Decatur Herald and Review (April 3, 2012) that supports negative word power, **"Cancer diagnosis can kill research finds."** Cancer can kill long before malignant tumors take their toll, new research shows. A study involving more than 6 million Swedes reveals that the risk of suicide and cardiovascular death increased immediately after a cancer diagnosis." Does this surprise anyone?

This article alarmingly reveals the power of a negative diagnosis. Also, these researchers stated, "They found that risk of suicide or cardiovascular death increased in the first few weeks after the diagnosis." What in the world are these cancer patients saying to themselves?

Whether we have a thought or a spoken word, the mind does not know the difference. As a result, whatever is positive or negative begins a **word circuit** running through each of us, affecting various parts of the body.

Matthew 4:4 Jesus asks, **"Are we living by bread alone or living by the words that proceed from the mouth of the Lord?"** When we do not know God's word to study it and show ourselves approved, then we are living by bread alone—this is man's word (such as a negative diagnosis).

Here is another thought. Remember that old saying **"Actions speak louder than words"?** Have you noticed that we are more word-oriented than we are action-oriented? In general, we are people that like to talk. We like to give words, share words, receive words, and even sling words when angry.

If we choose to change our thinking patterns and let God's word be our word, then our actions will match our words.

What About Me?

We defeat our own potential successes by the negative messages we give to ourselves. **It has been said we entertain 50,000 negative words a day.** Also, research reveals every person carries an inner dialogue with self which consists of **150-300 words a minute and 45,000 to 51,000 thoughts a day. We cannot go 11 seconds without self-talk.** Where does all this come from? Many of these negative messages come from unhealed hearts and others negative words that are still imbedded within us. These hurtful thoughts and words reveal our heart wounds.

How do these heart wounds continue their circuits of negativism in our bodies? Basically, we fight a constant war over negative thoughts. This continuing battle is all about keeping us from grasping what God's word says about us.

Our enemy, Satan, fills our minds with the negative events from our past. He is also the creator of all our fears. F.Y.I – futuristic fear is called anxiety. **When we are living in the past, we have a tendency to be depressed. When we are living in the future, we are usually in a state of anxiety.**

Our words bring forth life or death, and we must be aware of the death words that want to come out from within us. The comforter, Holy Spirit, will train us, equip us, propel us, and bless us to release energy words that will run their circuit from one end of the earth to the other, bringing forth life. These energy words will find God's believers struggling through spiritual issues, and will attach themselves to those seeking God's will and purpose for their lives. Then a spiritual uplifting will embrace them and help them in their journey.

On the other hand, a death word (negative) will do the same and attach itself to other negative words, and this keeps these words in a death word cycle, resulting in an oppressed, depressed state.

We must find a straight and narrow path to replace the crooked path we have been traveling in life.

I love God's grace and mercy. God knows that we have been deeply programmed to hear and absorb so much negativity that we are unable to catch God's words as they pour this into our mind and captivates our thought life.

The more we meditate on scriptures, the deeper the word goes within us. When the Lord quickens His word, stop right there and stay with that word for a while; **meditate on it, pray over it, ask God to give you more revelation on it**.

This is how the Lord seals His word in us, then allows it to go deep within us—**Deep calls to deep.**

For example, Proverbs 16:24 states, "Pleasant words are like honeycomb sweetness to the soul and health to the bones." These are healing words.

If we would start being more pleasing and more loving, pleasant, merciful, and graceful to ourselves, our bones, flesh, and cells would exhibit peace and bring forth the healing our bodies need. Our tongues definitely need to be disciplined and taught from wise leaders.

Tongue of the Learned

When I awake in the mornings, the first thing I think of and say is: **"The Lord God has given me the tongue of the learned. He awakens me morning by morning. He awakens my ears to hear as the learned."**

As one of His learned, my mind rolled around to think about one of the many chapters that I have a desire to write about. I thought about the book of Nehemiah and how God had called him to rebuild the ruined walls of the city. My mind wanders to the walls we build in our personal lives and how these walls begin to be built at an early age.

My youngest grandchildren, Piper and Mimi, ages four and five, are at such a wonderful, innocent age. In the near future, they, too, will learn to build a wall when someone hurts their feelings, makes fun of them, or harshly disciplines them in a way that they do not understand. I wish there was some way I could protect them from the negative words that they will endure through their developmental years. However, Christ said, "all things will work for the good of those who love the Lord." I will do all that is within my power to teach them to love the Lord. It will definitely be their protection. And mine, too.

Real Life, Real Time

Max Lucado wrote a book called **<u>You Are Special</u>**. It is about the Wemmicks who were small, wooden people, created by a carpenter named Eli. This is one of my favorite stories about how words affect us.

The book tells how each of the Wemmicks were different in every way. Every day, they were given a box of Golden star stickers and a box of Gray dot stickers. The good looking ones **"always got stars."** The others, that were not up to par, received gray dots.

A Wemmick called Punchinello was awkward and clumsy and fell a lot—he always accumulated dots. He ended up with so many dots he didn't want to do anything or go anywhere. He wanted no more dots. He met a female Wemmick named Lucia, and **"she had no dots or stars."** Lucia was admired and everyone wanted to give her stars. The problem was that even on Lucia, the Golden stars would always fall off.

She shared her secret that she would go see Eli the Woodmaker on a daily basis. She convinced Punchinello to go see Eli, and when he did, Punchinello found out from Eli how special he was. Eli also told him why the stickers did not stay on Lucia. Eli said it was about trust and love. Eli told Punchinello that **"you are special because I made you, and I don't make mistakes."**

The Wemmick, Punchinello with all the dots, said to himself, "I think Eli really means I am special," and with this profound thought, a dot fell to the ground. What an eloquent way to say that how we feel about ourselves and what others say about us has a profound effect on us.

Like attracts like, meaning whatever is within us will attract the same things that are in others. Our protection is to think on these things, **"Whatsoever things are true, whatsoever things are honest, whatsoever things are just, whatsoever things are pure, whatsoever things are lovely, whatsoever things are of a good report; if there be any virtue, and if there be any praise, think on these things" (Phillipians 4:8).**

This is what **real life in real time** is all about.

Check out the following Wemmick Prayer.

A Wemmick Prayer
I Am Special

Lord, thank you for showing me that my life is not a mistake. You made me out of the love that You are. You called me into being at the right time and the right place. You prepared a way for me and gave Your life for me. I am a privilege, not a burden; a joy and a delight, not an intrusion; I BELONG!! I am a treasure just because I am and not for what I can do. I am one of the Father God's children, and He delights in me. I'M SPECIAL! I'm a wonderful, lovable, likable person, so I can impact peoples lives and serve this generation according to Your will for my personal life.

Prayer for Sticks and Stones

My beloved Father,

You know my story. You're aware of all the negative words that have hurt me and bruised me. Your word promised, a bruised reed. You would not break and a smoking flax, You would not quench. I know You will never quench my flickering spirit.

Lord, I know You are passionate for me, and You will not break me when I'm bruised or broken. Your word states that Your tender mercies are new and fresh every morning. This word covers me when negative words are trying to attach themselves to me.

The cry of my heart is for your protection. I know Your hand lovingly holds me above negative attacks and Your ear always hears my cry. My cry now is wash me, cleanse me from all and any defiling words that have attached themselves to me from the past, and also those in the present.

Lord, I ask You to anoint my tongue so that I will not release any negative or defiling words from my own mouth. Anoint my tongue to release words to comfort, edify, and exhort myself and your beloved children.

Thank you Lord Jesus for Your amazing love for me.

A Word Declared Is Established

- I declare my ears are anointed to hear.
- I declare the word will not be taken out of my heart.
- I declare I will hide God's word in my heart.
- I declare God's word will take root in me.
- I declare God's word will not be choked out of me with the pleasures of life.
- I declare I will hear God's word with a noble and pure heart.
- I declare things will be established by my word.
- I declare I will hear God's word behind me saying: "this is the way, go ye in it."
- I declare these declarations will be established.

A reminder: Remember to speak out loud these declarations.

The Power of the Spoken Word

- **Proverbs 18:21** – "Death and life are in the power of the tongue, And those who love it will eat its fruit."

- **Proverbs 6:2** – "You are snared by the words of your own mouth; You are taken by the words of your mouth."

- **Proverbs 10:11** – "The mouth of the righteousness is a well of life, But violence covers the mouth of the wicked."

- **Proverbs 12:25** – "Anxiety in the heart of man causes depression, But a good word makes it glad."

- **Proverbs 16:24** – "Pleasant words are life a honeycomb, Sweetness to the soul and health to the bones."

- **II Samuel 23:2** – "The Spirit of the Lord spoke by me, And His word was on my tongue."

- **Jeremiah 15:16** – "Your words were found, and I ate them, And Your word was to me the joy and rejoicing of my heart; For I am called by Your name, O Lord God of hosts."

- **Jeremiah 23:29** – "Is not My word like a fire?" says the Lord, And like a hammer that breaks the rock in pieces?"

- **Psalm 107:20** – "He sent His word and healed them, And delivered them from their destructions."

- **Psalm 119:11** – "Your word I have hidden in my heart, That I might not sin against You."

- **James 3:10** – "Out of the same mouth proceed blessing and cursing. My brethren, these things ought not to be so."

- **Hebrews 4:12** – "For the word of God is living and powerful, and sharper than any two edged sword, piercing even to the division of soul and spirit, and of joints and marrow, and is discerner of the thoughts and intents of the heart."

His word changes my tongue.
Let His Word bring life to you, as it has done for me.

Is It Evil To Hate?

*To hate in the natural creates a root
of poison from within. To hate in the
spiritual brings forth judgment of sin.*
— Anita Mason 10/27/11

I am always looking diligently for a word from the Lord that quickens my spirit. When I find that word or that promise, then *something stirs deep within me,* then I begin to receive a deeper meaning to His word that I had not seen before.

When I'm reading, and an author excites me with insight on a subject, I put my book down so I can focus on digesting what I have read. In other words, I take a big gulp of something I love and let the rest of my body enjoy the download for a while. So, if you find yourself gulping while reading something that excites you, allow yourself to absorb the material by putting it aside for a few moments. Can anyone identify with this?

Keeping my need to download in mind, I am always looking diligently for a word from the Lord that quickens my spirit. When I find that word or that promise, something stirs deep within me, and I begin to receive a deeper meaning to His word that I had not seen before.

This is what happened to me, a deep stirring, when I meditated on Psalm 97:10, "You who love the Lord *hate* evil." He *preserves* the souls of his saints; He *delivers* them from the hand of the wicked. Holman Bible Dictionary describes hate as "*strong negative reaction; a feeling toward someone considered an enemy, possibly indicating volatile hostility*." The commentary shares that, as believers, we are to hate whatever opposes God. We are not to have a malicious attitude. Our *hate* of evil must reflect our agreement with God's opposition to evil. Many of the psalms may sound vindictive, but the ultimate punishment of the wicked is left to God's divine justice.

Our sense of honor is if we truly love the Lord, we will hate evil! When this is the genuine outflow of our heart, He *declares* in His word that *He will preserve the souls of His saints*. With this type of a declaration, our souls must be an important component to salvation. The Lord wants our whole being—spirit, soul and body—plugged into Him.Meaning our reasoning, power of intellect, choice and decisions to hate evil not the person. The demonic power of hate will drive a person.

Spirit of the Mind

Most of our traditional teaching consists of the spiritual man. God is revealing to us in the past, present, and future that our souls must be regenerated and come into alignment with our spirit. He states in His word to "*Be renewed in the spirit of your mind,*" also to "circumcise your heart." How can we circumcise our own hearts except through a decision of our *regenerated mind*? It must be our decision to cut out anything that would hold us back from His love.

What does our soul consist of? It is our mind, will, intellect, and emotion, plus our flesh that houses our spirit. Our Lord is telling us that our love of Him and hate for evil will assure us that He will preserve all the intricate parts of our being. How much plainer could God speak to us about *His love for our love*?

As if that was not enough, then the psalmist states: "He delivers them out of the hand of the wicked" Psalm 37:40. *What a promise that we can stand on.* This psalm moves on to state the hand of the wicked cannot hold me in bondage. In fact, I believe that God puts an invisible spiritual shield around us to protect us and keep us from the fiery darts of the enemy. Remember, *"He preserves the souls of His saints."* God confirms His word to us over and over again. If we don't get it one way, He will see that we get it in another way or another verse stating almost the same thing.

Where are the Idols?

All through scripture God showers us with His promises and blessings. He also gives us instructions and lets us know specifically what He expects of us and what He will or will not tolerate. The one thing from beginning to the end He will not tolerate is our idol worship or worship of other gods (I John 5:21). *Anything that we put before God (placing more importance on) is an* **idol**. This could be anything from family, friends, religion, and addictions, something in the environment, the atmosphere or Heavens. People will become like the god they worship. (Take this time to meditate on Psalms 115.)

It would take too much time and space to list all possible addictive idols. No need to, most of us know what idols we struggle with. What is our goal? *Love* the Lord, *hate* evil. I love what Psalm 34:15 tells us,

"The eyes of the Lord are on the righteous. And His ears are open to their cry." This tells me that God is listening for my cry. Verse 17 states, "The righteous cry out and the Lord hears and delivers them out of all their troubles." **He not only does this, but His eyes are always searching for us ... for me.**

Grab hold of this word of the Lord, "*For the eyes of the Lord run to and fro through the whole earth, to show Himself strong on behalf of those whose heart is loyal to Him*" (II Chron. 16:9). These promises are a gift from God that He activates within each of us when our love for Him is greater than our love for the things of this world. He truly preserves the souls of His saints. Jesus Christ is the same **yesterday, today,** and **forever**. Hebrews 13:8.

I *challenge* you to look diligently for words from the Lord that quicken your spirit. Let His promise of our spiritual inheritance stir up those deep rivers of living water that He said would pour out of us. *Embrace His love.*

Begin with the following prayer and declarations.

A CLEANSING PRAYER FROM IDOLS

Lord God, break every ungodly idol in me – any idols in my heart, my mind, my emotions, my spirit, my soul, or my body. I curse any ancestral roots of idols and cleanse myself with the power of Christ's blood. I declare I will finish my walk on Earth without idols. My idol is Jesus.

In His Name
Amen.

DECLARATIONS

Father, Your word says to love You and hate evil, and as a result, Your word promises You will preserve my soul and deliver me from the hand of the wicked.

As a result:

- *I declare I will fear no evil because You are with me.*
- *I declare You will not lead me into temptation but keep me delivered from the evil one.*
- *I declare I will not repay anyone evil for evil.*
- *I declare I will not be overcome by evil but overcome evil with good.*
- *Last but not least, I declare my hatred of anything will come into agreement with God's opposition to evil.*
- *My blessings to all who oppose evil and embrace God's love.*

God Ministers in the Night Season

A dream is insight into your future that has escaped from your past, manifested in the now.

– Anita Mason 10/07/12

Some dreams can alter the course of an entire life. Often a dream will reveal where we need a healing; we can also be healed in our dreams and during our dreams. I have experienced both: dreams that revealed I needed a healing and healings that occurred during my dreams.

Have you ever had an ongoing dream or a nightmare? I have experienced a nightmare that plagued me for over 25 years. I ponder this thought; the deep work that the Lord does in dreams is the reason that I am so fascinated with them. I have realized through many of my own dream experiences that *God ministers in the night season.*

When my children were out of grade school, I went back to school. I sensed the Lord directing me into a counseling field. As a result, I enrolled in two college classes: Basic English and Psychology. Little did I know how much I would find out about myself in a Basic English and Psychology class. In the English class, I had to write a paper on <u>Cause and Effect</u>. I chose to write about an ongoing nightmare that had plagued me a large portion of my life. I called this writing assignment *"A Disaster Lives On."*

A Disaster Lives On

Before I share the nightmare, there is a part of my early childhood I need to mention to help with the understanding of these nightmares

I was raised spiritually in a strict traditional church. During church and Sunday school, I was enlightened with hell, fire, and brimstone teachings. Much was shared on the book of Revelation. As a result of these teachings, I connected my bad dreams to my fear of being left behind when the world ends. The nightmare was about the sun, a ball of fire, hurling toward the earth and exploding on impact. Everything on Earth was caught on fire, and the inevitable happened, all the people and the world were on fire, at this point I would wake up startled and fearful. My fear in the dream was that the world would be burned up, and I would not be ready to go to heaven. Much of my earlier teachings were on the Book of Revelation. To a child, there is much distortion when hearing a topic like this. As a result, in the dream I remember begging God to save me and take me in the rapture (a doctrinal belief) before He let the sun explode on the earth. This nightmare plagued me up until the time I went back to school. The disaster I wrote about was a huge traumatic hospital fire I witnessed as a child. Little did I know the traumatic effect this hospital fire had on me. This childhood incident caused shock, pain, and fear to be hidden within me.

In 1949, St. Anthony Memorial Hospital in Effingham, IL (at this time a small town of approximately 9,000 people) burned to the ground. Over 70 people died as a result of this fire. The entire city was thrown into a state of sudden shock and panic. This was especially true of my family because we lived directly across the street from the hospital. It was about midnight when my sisters and I were suddenly awakened by our panicked parents who were trying not to alarm us. They were shoving blankets and pillows into our arms as they ushered us outside, away from the house and onto the lawn. My parents explained that our hospital was on fire and the sparks from the fire were dangerous and could cause our house to catch on fire.

I wasn't very big at nine years old, and as my sisters and I were wrapped up in blankets, I felt even smaller. Our eyes were opened wide to the horrendous scene around us. *The picture is still vivid in my mind.* The hospital was a fiery inferno. Cries and screams were coming from people on the upper floors of the flame filled building. The trapped people were trying to climb out of the windows to breathe clean air or to jump. Patients were screaming and begging for ladders to get out of the building; some were running down the street with their clothes on fire. My father was trying to help catch people jumping from windows and wrapping blankets around those escaping the fire. The scene was a nightmare. My parents were not able to comfort my sisters, and myself, because they were helping the burning and escaping victims.

My remembrance of this fear is still vivid in my mind; *this had to be the end of the world*. I was sure everything was going to keep burning until the whole world was on fire. Consequently, as a nine year old, my world wasn't very big and my neighborhood in Effingham was the extent of it. As a result of this

hospital fire, there were many aftershocks of this traumatic event that affected our community profoundly.

Trauma Release

I want to stay focused on the trauma of the fire
and the ongoing nightmares. When I look back over
this incident in my childhood, it is no wonder that
I had re-occurring nightmares. All those years the
trauma that was held in my memory and body, I was
trying to be healed. The only release my unconscious
had was through the nightmares. I never thought to
connect these ongoing bad dreams with the hospital
fire that had traumatized me as a child. My theory
was that I needed to be saved again and again. Since
I felt I did not have my act together spiritually, I was
burning up with the rest of the world.

As I was writing about this traumatic event
during my English class in 1984, I suddenly realized
that the nightmares were a result of unconscious
panic, fear, and shock that had been kept alive within
me due to the hospital fire I witnessed as a child. In
other words, when I wrote about this fire disaster,
it opened my revelation of the ongoing nightmares.
Several years before I had gone back to school, my
early childhood fear of the Lord had been healed, and

I had re-dedicated my life to the Lord. As a result of the disaster writing, the Lord was able to help me put all the pieces of a childhood trauma back together and heal my ongoing nightmare. Whether we are aware of it or not, we all have some degree of trauma locked within us. Trauma becomes a part of our chemistry. Unless we become aware that our bodies need to be released of the trauma, we carry that trauma until something symptomatic—spirit, soul, or body—reveals it. I was also healed from another traumatic incident in my childhood that involved emergency appendectomy surgery shortly after the hospital fire, causing compounded trauma.

These healings intensified my interest in dream understanding. Since that time, I have acquired a large collection of articles and books on Biblical dreams. I often teach and minister on dream under-standing. I have taught classes, given workshops and seminars, and I am still learning newer and deeper insights about dreams. Do I understand everything about dreams? No! I realize there are others more qualified than I to teach and speak on dreams.

There are a few basic things I want to write about pertaining to God's ministering power. One thing I feel certain of is that God created us in such a way that we are able to release all the conscious and unconscious material we gather through the day and night in our dreams. I might add, even old material from the past that is still attached to us is often released and healed. I call this material *unfinished business or earlier trauma.*

Dreams are God's way of ministering to us spiritually in our night seasons. There are over two hundred scriptures that give reference to dreams and visions. That is 1/3 of the Bible. When something is mentioned this many times in God's Word, it is very significant. I suggest we pay attention.

Here's a brief definition of a dream from my I Pad that states: *1. A dream is a succession of images, thoughts, or emotions passing through the mind during sleep; 2. The sleeping state in which this occurs.* In our dream state, some dreams come from secret desires, false information, or perversion that people put in their mind and spirit while they are awake – this affects their dreams and their physiology.

In reality, our dreams are nothing more than a different state of awareness. I might add another level of consciousness (often referred to as an altered state of consciousness). Dreams are inward oriented and more sensitive than wakefulness. Dreams are another way of letting us know where we are in our lives. The more I study to understand my life and my dreams,

the greater peace and understanding I will have interpreting my dreams and live a balanced life.

In ancient times, dreams were an important way
of seeking the future and making important decisions.
For example, religious and spiritual scholars that were
skilled in dream interpretation would be consulted on
governmental or kingdom issues when important or
dire decisions were needed.

In this early time period, *"dream books"* were
written to give understanding of dreams by symbols.
I mention this to show a comparison to what is happening now on our spiritual watch. Many spiritual
scholars that studied dreams and visions, some not
as spiritually qualified as others, have written dream
books. One whom I consider a qualified dream scholar
is John Paul Jackson. Some of these authors and dream
interpreters have been contacted by government offi-
cials for dream understanding. Even now, some of our
leading prophetic ministers are consulted by governmental leaders for decision making, and information
on future events, just like our prophets of old.

A God Cycle

This is an interesting cycle, God wanting once
again to reveal His passionate nature to His people

through dreams. Many of us know He has always wanted to reveal Himself to us. However, scripture tells us that our ears have been dulled and our vision clouded, resulting in a hindrance to dream interpretation.

Another scripture tells us that we look through a glass darkly (1 Corinthians 13:12). I believe this is a defining metaphor for much of Christianity today. We're not getting a clear picture of the depth that Christ wants us to know Him in. How do we do this? One of the ways is to allow God to open our understanding and speak to us again in the *language of dreams and even visions*.

The interesting cycle I mentioned is God revealed Himself through dreams and visions in the biblical ancient days, and He's doing it once again. What's that old cliché saying, *"what goes around comes around?"* Well, dreams and visions are here once again. Let's embrace all that God has for us.

When we embrace our dream nature that God created within us, we must also know and learn areas of caution. God always instructs us on how to discern good or evil in every provision of His Word intended for our spiritual growth. Dreams are often a mixture of things that are very spiritual and at the same time worldly. Through dreams we can see the blind spots in our lives, meaning things about ourselves that we are not aware of when we're awake.

One thing is certain: the creative part of us is from God. Some dreams may be filtered into our being by our own sinful nature, "Garbage in, garbage out," filtered through dreams. Our dreams filter out all kinds of things that we have been exposed to. In our sleep state, the filter is removed. This leaves us in an enhanced state of awareness susceptible to stimuli we would not usually notice.

For example, bodily sensations (the physiology I mentioned earlier) during our dream state may be revealing indigestion, full bladder, rising temperature, and such, is manifested in our dreams (maybe a bathroom break is needed). The thing we must consider is that we can also have physical problems or illnesses that are manifested through dreams. It's our body's way of trying to release what our consciousness does not want to know about ourselves, basically breaking through our denial systems. In case of any defiling dreams, we need to prayerfully cleanse ourselves. We encounter all types of defilement around us every day which affects us in the night season through our dreams.

Is every dream we have from God? It is my personal belief that every dream we have, good or bad, is created within us to speak to us, warn us, prophecy over us, heal us, or announce forthcoming events. On the other hand, negative and alarming dreams, even seducing dreams, are our bodies way of telling us we have a problem or possibly a sin nature that gives us no peace and needs to be dealt with, meaning some type of healing is needed. All these types of dreams, positive or negative, are God's creative mechanism in mankind for us to be encouraged, healed, delivered, or convicted.

Healing Dreams

Speaking of our body consciousness, there is another release through dreams – personal trauma. This is the mind's way of releasing what is not consciously known by the person who experienced the trauma. For example, remember the ongoing nightmare that I started this chapter with? The body has everything it needs to heal itself. My body, mind, and spirit were trying to release the trauma through the nightmares. I was not getting the answer because I knew nothing about how dreams work. However, God is faithful. "He found a way where there was no way" to heal me.

I mentioned I had two healings during dream time that when I awakened I knew I was healed. I saw the healing in the dream, walked through it, and awakened to know I was healed.

One such healing was a brief dream or vision, I'm not quite sure. Someone was pushing something across my forehead, deep and with great pressure. I knew something significant was happening. They applied several deep strokes across my head, then during the dream or vision, it was stated that I was having spiritual surgery. I was instantly awake and knew that some type of spiritual healing had occurred physically and mentally.

These are just some of the experiences revealing what God does in our dreams or visions which are interchangeable in the Old Testament. One other question that is often asked is, "Why does God allow the enemy to torment us during the night season?" God does not allow this to happen. We cause these tormenting things to occur by what we see, do, or experience in our daily lives. What we deal with through the day will be revealed in the night. **"A wise man will hear and increase learning, And a man of understanding will attain wise counsel, to understand a proverb and an enegma, The words of the wise and their riddles.** *(Proverbs 1:5-6).* If we apply this scripture, it will help give us wisdom and insight to untangle parables and dreams.

In the Old Testament and New Testament, God gave us a symbol system that He wanted us to use and study for a guideline to interpret dreams. If we study His system, He will honor it and use it to communicate with us. For example, dreams, visions, metaphors, parables, and Biblical stories are God's symbol system for interpreting dreams. This is what I want. How about you?

I believe Those who study and meditate on God's Word will have a clearer understanding in their dreams. This is opposed to those whose minds are filled with television, video games, mythology, pagan literature, and such. If we study and soak ourselves in scripture, slowly over time we will find that our dreams will be one of the vehicles that God will use to communicate His language to us. One example is found in Job 33:14-18, telling us how God uses dreams to keep us from perishing. Check these insightful scriptures out. The Bible does not say that all dreams come from God. It does not say that all dreams are spiritual, but the word is clear that we are susceptible to spiritual messages. In other words, dreaming is a state in which messages may be received while we sleep.

Ultimately, God created our dream state within us to give us a deep insight for healing and restoration and also to bring new awareness to the things we dismiss, internalize, and disconnect ourselves from. The Lord wants us to be complete in Him—spirit, soul, and body (I Thessalonians 5:23).

I have a dream journal that I keep track of significant dreams with. I have journaled for many years, not only dreams, but spiritual insights from God's word. It would be my recommendation for you to journal your dreams and revelations. When journaling, you will also discover how God uses dreams to keep us from perishing *because what God does in the nighttime, He reveals in the daytime for our healing.*

Be blessed with these following scriptures that confirm God ministers in the night season.

God Ministers in the Night Season

Job 35:10 But no one says, Where is my God my Maker, Who gives songs in the night,

Psalm 16:7 I will bless the Lord who has given me counsel; My heart Also instruct me in the <u>night</u> seasons.

Psalm19:2 Day unto day utters speech, And <u>night</u> unto <u>night</u> reveals knowledge.

Psalm 30:5 ....Weeping may endure for a <u>night</u>, But joy comes in the morning.

Psalm 42:8 The Lord will command His loving kindness in the daytime, and in the <u>night</u> His song shall be with me....

Psalm 77:6 I call to remembrance my song in the <u>night</u>; I meditate within my heart, And my spirit makes diligent search.

Psalm 119:55 I remember Your name in the <u>night</u>, O Lord, and I keep Your law.

Psalm 139:11 If I say, "Surely the darkness shall fall on me," Even the <u>night</u> shall be light about me.

Isaiah 21:11 He calls to me out of Sier, "Watchman, what of the <u>night</u>? Watchman, what of the <u>night</u>?"

John 19:39 And Nicodemus, who at first came to Jesus by <u>night</u>...

Prayer for Receiving Dreams and Visions

Dear Heavenly Father,

In Joel chapter two, Your Word says, "You will pour out Your Spirit on all flesh." You said in verse 28 and 29, "And it shall come to pass afterward that I will pour out My Spirit upon all flesh; Your sons and Your daughters shall prophesy, Your old men shall dream dreams, Your young men shall see visions. And also on My menservants and on My maidservants I will pour out My Spirit in those days."

Heavenly Father, pour Your Spirit out upon me that I will prophesy, that I will dream dreams and have visions — on my bed in the night seasons and through the day. Release those dreams and visions you have already birthed within me. I'm not going to let go of these dreams and visions until You bring them to pass.

I can do this because in Isaiah 41:21 You state, "present your case". Bring forth your strong reasons." Well, Lord, I am stating my case and bringing forth my strong reason that You will minister to me through my dreams.

Heavenly Father, Your word states that You will pour Your Spirit upon all flesh. This is my promise, my inheritance, and <u>I receive it now</u>.

I decree and declare this is my season to walk in Your Spiritual enlightenment of dreams and visions and the understanding to interpret them.

I say, <u>do it NOW, Lord</u>—release Your Holy Spirit upon me.

The Father's Ministry Over Me

I Declare: *I will swim with reckless abandon in the deep and hidden things of God.*

I Declare: *My eyes will see God moving in every situation.*

I Declare: *My Father will teach me to recapture and learn the language of symbols, metaphors, signs, and wonders.*

I Declare: *My God will give me dreams, visions, and prophetic impressions.*

I Declare: *My Father will let me see the world through His eyes, and I will understand His symbolic language, signs, and actions.*

I Declare: *My Father will teach me how to live with my eyes "wide open" to be able to see and experience His presence in every area of my life, especially in the night season.*

I Declare: *God will never let me lose the wonder of how He speaks to me and how I fit into His divine plan, morning, noon, and nighttime, too.*

Proverbs 25:2 It is the glory of God to conceal a matter; to search out a matter is the glory of kings.

Father, I eagerly look forward to go with You where You take me in the Spirit.

I believe for God's waves of Glory!!!

                      Be Blessed in nighttime healing.
                                  Anita

The End at the Beginning

A cycle is a beginning that has no end, and an end that has no beginning, what was is now, and what is now, is what was.

– Anita Mason 11/14/12

Somehow, I pictured this chapter at the end of the book when really it should probably be at the beginning. However, it will be toward the end because I want my readers to give some serious thought to this chapter.

A couple of years ago, I was asked to teach and minister at a weekend retreat. I was very honored to be asked, and I began immediately to think about what the Lord might want me to share. The person who asked me to do the retreat already had a theme. This helped me search out my topics. As I prayed about how the weekend teaching was to be, I knew my focus was (as always) on how the Lord wanted me to end the two day teaching. I continued asking the Lord about what I was to share. I repeatedly heard this phrase *"Do the End at the Beginning."* The more I studied and put together this teaching, the stronger *The End at the Beginning* message was formulating for the retreat. I knew what the Lord meant because of my earlier concerns pertaining to ministry.

As a result, I had a new awareness of what the phrase *"End at the Beginning"* meant. In the past, I have had much apprehension (followed by prayer) over the heavy portion of ministry that is left to the end of Christian meetings. Why? Because from what I have observed, usually all the deeper type of ministry, praying, deliverance, laying on of hands, etc. is ministered at the end.

When attendees leave these spiritual gatherings, many are still open and vulnerable. Often there has been no closure after their spirits have been opened. This means that a person's spirit is opened more toward the end of the meeting, and this leaves them spiritually vulnerable. Most ministries do not have follow-up to help with those that have been opened up and need more healing or some type of closure before leaving.

A couple of years ago, I wrote in my journal that *"I have found I am doing things backward. I was doing the end at the beginning."* I also wrote, *"It seems like the heavy or deep things that need to be dealt with needed to be addressed first so I can breeze through the rest of the ministry."*

> *I have declared the former things from the beginning; they went forth from my mouth and I caused them to hear it. Suddenly I did them and they came to pass. (Isaiah 48:3)*

The above scripture gave me the confidence to go into the deeper things of the Lord at the beginning of my meetings and then give the participants more process time and no waiting until the end to tend to personal ministry.

About the same time I received a confirming scripture that stated *"Declaring the end from the beginning, and from ancient times things that are not yet done (Isaiah 46:10).* This scripture also confirmed what I was struggling with pertaining to ministry. It was my ok from God.

In summary, let's not save the good or heavy ministry for the last and consider to begin the ending at the beginning of what's on your heart to share. By the time the participants are ready to leave, they will have processed much of the teaching and will not leave open and vulnerable to their own wounds or wounds of others.

I realize this chapter might be a little harder to understand from my perspective. However, as a clinician, I am always concerned about what state a person leaves in, whether it be ministry or counseling. Healing is the ultimate goal for our spirit, soul, and body. When people leave a meeting, we want to know that they are ok and leaving stronger than when they arrived.

I welcome comments on this
particular chapter on ministry timing.
Thank you,

Anita

A Beginning and an Ending Prayer For You

Father, this is one of the chapters that I need more insight and revelation. I am asking that You illuminate my spirit man and help me to understand what I have need of.

Wherever I go or whatever I do, I ask for Your divine protection over me, especially if I minister to others or they minister to me.

I choose to leave every meeting, retreat, or connection with others healthier and stronger than I arrived and with your protection.

Holy Spirit, I trust you to be with me in every situation, whether I'm giving or receiving, to know Your loving hand of favor is upon me.

In Jesus' name
Amen

This would be a good prayer to pray just before receiving any type of teaching or ministry.

Anita

Let's Declare What God is Telling Us

- *I declare the Holy Spirit will protect me through every healing that I may need.*
- *I declare my spiritual perception will not be distorted.*
- *I declare I will not presume I have arrived.*
- *I declare I desire truth in my inward parts.*
- *I declare I will study to show myself approved to know the difference between truth and the spirit of error.*
- *I declare I will not allow isolation in me to breed deception.*
- *I declare when I bind the strongman, he will not rule and reign in my life.*

Christ will govern my life for such a time as this
– Selah!

The following song confirms my passion to write and share with you the value and the importance of a Spiritual Blessing.
This is my story; this is my song.

BLESSED ASSURANCE

Blessed Assurance, Jesus is mine
O what a foretaste of glory divine
Heir of salvation, purchase of God
Born of His Spirit, and washed in His blood
Perfect submission, all is at rest
I in my Savior am happy and blessed
Watching and waiting, looking above
Filled with His goodness, lost in His love

This is my story, this is my song
Praising my Savior all the day long
This is my story, this is my song
Praising my savior all the day long

Perfect submission, perfect delight
Visions of rapture now burst on my sight
Angels descending bring from above
Echoes of mercy, whispers of love

This is my story, this is my song
Praising my Savior all the day long
This is my story, this is my song
Praising my Savior all the day long

Lyrics by: Fanny Crosby

Assured Blessings

Psalm 68:19 Blessed be the Lord who daily loadeth us with benefits even the God of our salvation. Selah.

The Power of a Blessing

One of the greatest revelations I have ever received from the **Word of the Lord** is the **Power of the Blessing**. It is a powerful, insightful, and revelatory promise from the Lord. My prayer is that I can do anointed justice to this chapter.

My passion for writing about the blessing is because of its spiritual impact upon the earth and mankind. For example, in the beginning when God blessed what He created, it released a power and spiritual energy over whatever it touched. When a blessing is spoken (whatever it is spoken over), the very DNA of its substance is impacted and changed. I discovered the power of a blessing when I received a *Father* and a *Mother blessing* at a seminar 15 years ago. From that time on, blessing others has been a way of life for me.

In *My Father's House Healing Room,* a *"Blessing"* is used more than any other prayers. Why? Because our healing team knows the power of a blessing – it comforts, edifies, and exhorts. It also ushers us into a new level of maturity which is one of the most important components of the spoken blessing. I'll have more on this later. The Bible has much to say about blessings. In fact, the word bless or blessing occurs over 400 times in scripture.

First of all, what is a blessing and when did it originate? Webster's Dictionary defines a blessing as "a prayer or solemn wish imploring happiness upon another; a benediction or blessing; the act of pronouncing a benediction or blessing; that which promotes prosperity and welfare." To bless means to invoke divine favor on, to bestow happiness, prosperity, or good things of all kinds; to make a pronouncement holy; to consecrate, to glorify for the benefits received, to extol for Excellencies.

Our Father in heaven loves to *bless His children.* It is my belief that the blessing that was *imparted from the Father* is a powerful spiritual principle that God released in His word. As a result, we, in turn, *can impart* the Father's blessing to others.

The first spoken blessing was by God as He spoke creation into being. *"And God created the sea monsters and every living creature that moves with which the water swarmed after their kind. And every winged bird after its kind; and God saw it was good. And God blessed them saying be fruitful and multiply."* Genesis 1:21-22

Be Fruitful and Multiply

From the very beginning, God used the spoken blessing to fulfill His plan for creation. God used the power of His words with the creative force behind them to bless what he brought into existence. Adam and Eve were to serve as God's representative in the earth—having been formed in His image. They had a *body, soul, and spirit* in the pattern or likeness of the Holy Trinity. *Let's declare together* that "*all my parts are in the likeness of God*" (Father, Son and Holy Spirit).

The second blessing was spoken over Adam and Eve. So, God created man in His own image...And God blessed them, and God said, "*Be fruitful and multiply and replenish the earth*" (Genesis 1:27-28).

And *a third blessing* was given in Genesis 9:1. God made a covenant with Noah and blessed him and his sons and said to them, *"Be fruitful and multiply and replenish the earth."* It is interesting to note that when God blessed, He added be fruitful and multiply and replenish the earth. His message continues at this present time. His word from beginning to end is *"be fruitful and multiply."*

Abraham's Descendants

In Isaiah 51:2, we are commanded to "Look to Abraham your father and to Sarah who bore you: For I called him alone, and blessed him and increased him." *Abraham, our earthly Father, was God's choice to bring forth His blessing to all nations.* God chose a man who would know and serve Him faithfully. From Abram's (later named Abraham) family, a chosen nation of people would be separated unto Him. *These are the four blessings the Lord declared over Abraham and his descendants.* (Genesis 12:2-3)

I will bless You
And You will be a blessing
I will bless them that bless You
And in You all the families of the earth
Will be blessed.

This powerful blessing over Abraham is still active and electrically charged with spiritual energy (to this day) to continue to bless all nations. *We are the descendants of Abraham.* This blessing is mine and yours. This purpose has now been accomplished through Christ. He brought forth the Old Testament blessings and taught His disciples their spiritual value to be woven into the new covenant.

The Lord commanded Moses to teach Aaron to bless. God gave Moses a blessing he wanted spoken over His people as they assembled together. This blessing is known among the Jewish people as the *"High Priestly Blessing."* This is the blessing that Aaron spoke over the sons of Israel.

Numbers 6:24-27 – "The Lord told Moses to speak to Aaron and his sons, saying this is how you will bless the children of Israel. Say to them:

The Lord bless you and keep you;
The Lord make His face shine on you and be gracious to you;

*The Lord lift His countenance on you and give
you peace.*
*"So they shall invoke My name on the sons of
Israel. And I will bless them."*

To "*invoke*" means to bless, to call for a blessing,
to put into use, or to call forth.

Stagger Not

In the New Testament, the practice of a blessing
was released on a regular basis among the Jewish
people. In fact, even to this day, The *Father
blessing* is released in the Jewish household every
Friday.

In the Book of Ruth, a blessing is released over
Jewish daughters. Even today, these parents often
pray, "*The Lord make the women that is coming
to your house like Rachel and Lea, the two who
built the house of Israel.*" From these two women
came the 12 tribes of Israel. This blessing from Ruth
4:11-12 was spoken from the heart of the Jewish
people over Ruth. Jewish Fathers love to speak this
blessing over their daughters, and they often end the
prayer with "*and be famous in Bethlehem,*" just like
it was released in the Old Testament.

Jesus himself trained His disciples to bless. Right after Jesus was tempted in the wilderness (Matthew 4), He began His ministry by teaching His disciples *The Beatitudes* (Matthew 5). These blessings are called *"The Sermon On The Mount."* Christ's sermon is about man's requirement to receive God's blessings for *Kingdom Living* on earth.

It is our responsibility to search the scriptures and find the promises that bless our children and ourselves when needed. God honors His word and every scriptural blessing that is spoken over His people. *Abraham "staggered not at the promises of God"* (Romans 4:19). Isn't it our responsibility to follow our forefather's spiritual pathways? I have often prayed the prayer that I would never *"stagger"* at God's promises to me. *"Let's Declare I will not stagger at God's promises to me."*

The declarations that we make using scripture are one of our ways of blessing our Lord and Savior. He loves to hear us speak His word back to Him. He also loves hearing our names and their spiritual meanings.

Parental Blessing

Our names are sealed within us from the moment that name is assigned to us, before or after birth. Just like the names in the Old Testament, our names have significant meaning. When we name our children, it would be in the best interest of the child for us to know the meaning of the name before it is given. Why? Because that name is so important and powerful that the child will gravitate toward its meaning. *A name is a special blessing from a parent that identifies their child and often propels them into their future.*

In our Healing Room, we tell those we pray for the meaning of their name. Then we share with them that when we or others speak their name, they are blessed with the meaning of that name. For example, my name, Anita, means grace or graceful one. When anyone calls me by name, they are really saying, Hi Anita, graceful one. I love the double meaning of my name.

Once we understand the depth of the meaning of our names, then we will have a spiritual understanding that a gravitation toward that name's meaning is inevitable. Before going any further, check out your God-given name and its meaning. You will be surprised that the characteristics of your name are already evident in your life. Names are meant to be a blessing. The Hebrew definition of *"to bless"* means ***Barach***. ***Barach*** means to kneel down before someone. The spiritual meaning is ***to empower or to prosper***. Our names are meant to empower us.

When a parent blesses his son or daughter, ***they are declaring they are empowered to prosper***. This means to prosper the whole person—spirit, soul, and body—along with material blessings. The greatest blessing a child can have is a father who blesses. The father is the one who helps birth all of the future dreams of the child. The love of a parent is so strong that it releases spiritual energy into their children. If the child is blessed at the age of puberty (which is usually around thirteen and according to their developmental maturity), this ushers them into a future that ***blesses them*** to ***thrive***, to ***prosper***, to ***succeed professionally,*** and to ***grow into adulthood*** in a mature and balanced manner. ***Basically, the blessing brings sons and daughters into maturity.***

Children that do not have fathers to bless them may struggle with immature behavior for a lifetime. I might add that if our teenagers had a parental blessing at significant stages of their development, especially at puberty, we would see less rebellion, troubled teens, and high risk behavior.

217

The Fatherless Generation

It has been stated that we are living in a time and season of a Fatherless generation. One of the biggest problems is there is no father figure to bless our sons and daughters. Many children are being raised without their father in the home. Adults that have been raised without a father in the home or the father was not there for them, in some manner, have had to parent themselves as children.

Those children are still struggling (as adults) emotionally *with an orphan mentality, which means they have the heart of an orphan*. These persons are often independent, self-reliant, insecure, and lack peace. Another characteristic is they strive for the praise and approval of others. They are all bound up in self-rejection and have problems with authority. It's not uncommon for them to seek comfort in surface relationships. This is called orphan mentality because of their disconnection or lack of feeling connected to others. Trying to always connect with someone, they feel they don't belong anywhere.

The lack of fathering and the lack of positive affirmation (blessing) has caused identity and self esteem problems in many of our children. These children have not been allowed to have a normal childhood due to neglect or over responsibility, resulting in that orphan feeling. Most parents are not aware of the power of a blessing, which results in parents withholding their blessing because they lack knowledge or understanding of its power.

There is a Jewish ceremony called ***Bar mitzvah*** that Jewish parents perform for their children at the time of puberty. This ceremony spiritually ushers that son or daughter into ***manhood or womanhood***. It also ***seals their identity*** in themselves, family, and community (another reason why our names are important). This blessing is futuristic. It propels the child towards a successful marriage, fruitfulness in child bearing, finances, their profession, health, and ministry calls.

This spoken blessing calls forth those things that are not as though they are (Romans 4:17), so that when a blessing is spoken over them, what exists in the future will be brought into existence.

God's Time

The words spoken in a blessing are powerful. It will often call things that are in the future into the now. ***Remember, the heavens and God's time is not*** *the same as our time. Our time is framed into the existence of this world. God's time is framed in the existence of Eternity.* He can bring anything out of eternity and place it just where he chooses in our time.

But God likes us to choose when we need something (if it is in His word) and call it forth. Since the beginning, God has given us all the authority we need to call forth and fulfill our *lifetime destiny* on this earth. This all began in Genesis (as I have already noted) when *God spoke His first blessing.* God spoke a blessing over mankind in order for us to continue this spiritual pathway. *God stated in His word that what has been blessed cannot be cursed.*

Who Can Bless?

In the New Testament, Christ is teaching us to override any curse by speaking blessings even to our enemies. This releases us for *unlimited types of blessings.* For example, I saved an article out of the newspaper (May 12, 2012, Decatur, IL). In a bold heading it stated, *"Blessing of the Horses Kicks off Summer Events."* A Christian organization planned a summer activity with the **Blessing of the Horses Service**. Animals are a blessing to many and can be blessed. *Bless your animals.*

Here is another interesting blessing. We love to vacation in Florida. As a result, we receive the **Destin Log Community Newspaper**. On June 4-7, 2011 in the Calendar of Events section of the newspaper, in bold letters was the *Blessed* and under this heading it stated *"Blessing of the Marketplace Draws Politicians, Realtors, and Responder."* Pastors and local church leaders had gathered together to bless Destin's businesses. This is what I would like to see done in our city. Another type of blessing is the *Priestly Blessing*. Do we have to be a priest to do this? Emphatically, no! Peter stated that we are a *"chosen generation, a royal priesthood..."* (1 Peter 2:9). We have been given the authority to function as a priest, and this is not gender specific. When we give a blessing, we are operating in a *"royal priesthood."* It was common practice in the New Testament church for the Jewish people to release a blessing. Jesus himself was all about blessing His disciples, the children, and those He ministered to.

There is also a *Servant Blessing*. 2 Samuel 7:29 says, *"Now therefore let it please you to bless the house of your servant, that it may continue forever before thee: For thou, O Lord God has spoken it and with thy blessing let the house of thy servant be blessed forever."*

Anyone serving us in any capacity may be blessed by us. We are also servants to the Lord and blessing ourselves is in order. *Jabez* called upon the God of Israel to bless him and enlarge his land and keep him from evil. God will bless us as we faithfully call upon Him. This is how we defeat evil. I am reminded of David and how he served Saul before He became King. David celebrated when the *Ark of the Covenant* was escorted back to Jerusalem. David assigned worshippers to worship and praise God for His presence. It was at this time that "He blessed the people in the name of the Lord of Hosts," and returned home to *Bless his household* (II Samuel 6:18).

David was a man after God's own heart, and his family blessing from the Father confirmed this. In case you're not aware of it, God is a family man. His heart is all about us.

Heart Blessing

With this thought in mind, I also believe there is a *Heart Blessing*. Matthew 5:8 says, *"Blessed are the pure in heart for they shall see God."* Our hearts are pure when we are able to have an emotional release from home from our parents. Leaving home is tied to blessing. When our hearts have not been blessed to leave, we will still be bound to our mothers and fathers. Many people in their 20's, 30's, 40's, etc. are still bound to mom and dad and have not cut the emotional umbilical cord. This just means you haven't fully matured because a part of you is still at home. Even Abraham (in the Old Testament) was told **"to get out of your country, from your family and from your Father's house, to a land that I will show you."** God blessed Abraham to leave his home. Genesis 12:1.

Parents hold the key to emotional release when they are able to bless their children and prophesy blessings unto their future. What can we do? We can bless our own hearts to be pure. We can bless our hearts to have the same attitude of the heart that God has. *Ask God to create in you a clean heart and bring this into existence.* There is no way that I can know or have full understanding of all the ways God has provided to bless us through Christ and for us to bless Him and others. This is one of those *"Launch Out Into the Deep"* to gain and discern more comprehension of this spiritual word *Bless*.

One more blessing I would like to mention is the *Grandparent Blessing* (this is my season in life). In Genesis 48, Jacob, in his seasoned twilight years, challenged himself to rise up in his weakened state to give special attention to his two grandsons. These children were Joseph's children that had been brought to see their grandfather because he wanted to bless them. Jacob blessed them as his own. He imparted a blessing to his grandchildren that is still in motion today by Jewish fathers speaking blessings over their sons. Blessings are spoken futuristic words that are still actively ushering in God's Kingdom on earth.

When To Bless

Grandparents are a special blessing in a child's life, and their importance is highly understated. As a result of the Biblical examples (many of them), one of the roles of the grandparent is to bless. I bless my grandchildren every opportunity I get.

When is the annointed spoken blessing usually given? Any time God's Spirit prompts you to bless, do so. His spirit knows what a person needs and when they need it. Even if you don't understand the depth and magnitude of the blessing, follow the spirit's leading. Remember, God's ways and thoughts are higher and greater than ours. *Spoken Blessings* do change people's futures. For this reason, let's look for and anticipate God to provide opportunities for us to bless others.

The Blessing

When a blessing is given, here is my suggestion. There is much stated biblically about the right hand. My intention is not to provide in depth information about the right hand. However, the right hand is what our Jewish forefathers used to impart a blessing. Remember, Christ is seated at the right hand of the Father, and Jacob used his right hand to bless his grandchildren. In the Healing Room, when we impart a blessing (especially father, mother blessings), we always use the right hand, placing it on the forehead or the top of the head. *Words are powerful and futuristic.* That is why we gravitate toward what is spoken. After a blessing has been released, it is always in order to speak prophetic words to whom you're blessing. When a Spiritual Father gives you a blessing;

> *Their role is to create (Genesis 1:27)*
> *Fathers give you an identity (Proverbs 22:1)*
> *Fathers protect (Hebrew 13:17)*
> *Fathers bless and Send (Genesis 29:25)*
> *Father's Prophesy into their Children's future (Genesis 49)*

This chapter ends with ***Father Blessing, God's Blessing, Why you can Bless with Authority, and Declarations.***

Father Blessing

My (Son/Daughter), it is my God given authority to anoint you and Bless you. Children are a gift from God, and when you were born, I acknowledged the gift that God had given me (us).

God's word stated that you were wonderfully and fearfully made. Your substance was fashioned by your Heavenly Father. Your assigned name is also a blessing. It defines who you are and the future God has prepared for you.

My Son/Daughter, I celebrate your life with you. You have blessed me with your existence. It is my desire that you prosper in all you are and in all you do. That spiritual blessing will be multiplied in your present and future.

Through all your developmental years, I have loved you all your life. I've seen your strength and weaknesses and loved you through each of them.

You have never been out of my thoughts. My love is with you and surrounds you.

I pray that God will surround you with His presence and release health and healing in every part of your life. I pray that God meets your every need and that you hold His love in your heart.

I pray that your future will hold loving and close friendships and that you would always choose people who would care for you, celebrate you, and honor you.

I pray that whatever important choices that you make in the future will be equally yoked with God's principles.

My prayer is that you will now be blessed into a new level of maturity. That spiritually, mentally, and emotionally you will become the adult the Father created you to be.

I bless you as a (male/female). I bless your (femininity/masculinity) and secure your gender identity into your God given future. I now impart this blessing that will complete your journey into spiritual maturity.

I seal this with the love of the father.

In Jesus Name, Amen

God's Blessing
To Release Over Others

Genesis 28:

May God Almighty bless you and make you fruitful and multiply you.

May God give you the dew of heaven and the fatness of the earth that you may be His assembly of peoples.

May the blessing of Abraham be given to you and your descendants, that you may inherit the land in which you occupy. I pray that your territory be increased and multiplied. And I pray the same blessing upon you that God gave to Abraham, Isaac and Jacob, and that the Angel of the Lord be with you to guard you and protect you.

I declare the Lord will make a way where there was no way and all your crooked paths be made straight and your destiny be fulfilled.

Selah! I seal this Blessing

Breaking Unhealthy Loyalty Ties

Father, give me a revelation of the depth that my family loyalty ties have kept me in bondage. I have been deceived into living my life in the shadows of my parents and all my ancestors. These shadows consist of conscious and unconscious unhealthy loyalty ties to my family of origin. This includes thoughts, behaviors, and actions I have received from these family patterns. Many of my unhealthy loyalty ties have come from ancestral blood lines somehow imparted to me, and many are destructive.

Lord, I now put the power of the blood and cross between me and my family and all my ancestors. I break all loyalty ancestral ties between me and them. I will no longer be in bondage to the past nor any family loyalty ties that have been imparted to me from generation to generation. Lord, I am aware that many loyalty blood ties are good, along with the unhealthy blood ties. I want to be free from good and bad loyality ties and choose to be connected to you and for You to mold me and shape me.

Thank you, Father, for setting me free from all family loyalty ties. You are a *God of Wonder and Awe* to set me free (once and for all) from all unseen spiritual ties to the past.

Selah

Your Unchained Child

Why You Can Bless With Authority
Here are your scripture confirmations:

1. II Cor. 5:21   You are the **righteousness** of God.

2. I John 4:4   **Greater** is He that is in you.

3. Luke 10:19   You have **authority** over all the **power** of the enemy.

4. John 14:12   **Greater works** than these shall you do.

5. Phil. 4:19   Your God will **supply** all your needs.

6. Heb. 4:16   You can come **boldly before** the throne of God.

7. Rom. 8:37   You are more than a **conqueror**.

8. Isaiah 54:17   No **weapon formed** against you can prosper.

9. Eph 6:16   You are able to **extinguish** all the fiery darts assigned to hurt you.

10. I Cor. 15:57 You are a **victor** not a **victim**.

11. Rom. 16:20 Your enemy is <u>under</u> your **feet**.

12. Col. 2:10 You are the **head** not the **tail**.

13. Mark 11:23 You can move **mountains**.

14. I John 2:27 Because you have an **anointing.**

These scriptures are an opportunity for you to use your authority to bless. Remember, the Lord loves to have his word spoken back to him.

Declare With Me

- I declare, Lord, You as the source of all my blessings.
- I declare I will be fruitful and multiply.
- I declare, Lord, that Your blessings over me have kept me in alignment with You.
- I declare as a result of Your promises to bless me, I have come into a new level of maturity.
- I declare fully that I want to bless You, and You have blessed me by speaking your word over others.
- I declare Your countenance is upon me, and I receive Your favor and peace.
- I declare as a result of the blessings You have released, I can have Kingdom living on Earth.
- I declare my name in a blessing, and my identity is secure because I am highly favored by my Father in Heaven.

Genesis 12:2 You shall be a blessing.
Psalm 129:8 blessing of the Lord be upon you.
I Peter 3:9 We were called to inherit a blessing.

"My Blessings for You"

May the Lord's Holy Spirit flow through you, filling every nook and cranny, meeting every need in your life.

May you know the height, breath, width, and depth of His love for you.

May you experience His tender mercies which are new and fresh every morning.

May His joy fill you and overflow through you onto others.

May others hear the words of Christ as you speak blessings of encouragement and truth: words which are seasoned with grace.

May you look upon the hills of your city and notice that they are white and ripe for harvest.

May you not be ashamed of the gospel of Jesus Christ, ready, in season and out, to share the love of Christ with others.

In Jesus' name, Amen.

The Mystery
What Is The Mystery Of
A Blessing?

I believe the Mystery of the Blessing is a deep spiritual revelation of the *atomic power* released when a blessing is spoken over someone or something. *All the spiritual forces from the kingdom of heaven are encapsuled in a blessing*. The revelation is not known nor given except through the Holy Spirit. The depth of our revelation will be the depth of the spiritual power ignited when the blessing is given.

The word says *deep calls to deep*; it is a deep earthly *mystery* to see the blessing propel people into their destiny. And we still do not have the understanding of how the spirit world moves to bring into existence the spoken word.

Another way to explain the *Mystery of the Blessing* is that it is unexplainable because it is a spirit work. It is a God given principle that was created when mankind was created. It is such a spiritual force that no man can claim nor tame it. It is only released by the spoken word that God put into place at creation. The key to this spiritual force is the spoken word. *God's blessing must be spoken out loud* and allowed to enter into humanity and also our environment. Why? Because the word states, *"Death and life are in the power of the tongue, and those who love it will eat its fruit"* Proverbs 18:21. Our love for God's blessing will be the fruit we eat thereof.

When God gave us authority over the land, sea, and air (Genesis 1), He also gave us the authority to bless and see whatever we bless to blossom and prosper *because anything we bless we are overriding evil*. If we, as God's representation on earth, do not walk in the revelation of what God has provided for us – *The blessing* – then we have missed a spiritual component of God's creation.

This is God's blessing that has been passed on from the beginning of our time when God first blessed creation. And when we walk in the revelation of it, we are *connected to God from creation to the present,* and the curse that was released on the earth no longer applies to God's saints that walk in the spiritual revelation of *The blessing*.

This is my belief why the *blessing is a mystery*. I believe that God through Christ wanted us to *unravel this mystery* and use it for kingdom living on earth. *What an atomic power the blessing is*. Is there any other power on earth any stronger than *the blessing*?

> *Genesis 12:2 "And I will make thee a great nation, and I will bless thee, and make thy name great; and thou shalt be a blessing."*

Did You Know?

Did you know?

That the spirit of man is the candle of the Lord, searching out all the innermost parts of the belly.

Did you know?

That no matter what the crisis or problem is, we have the true answer deep within us—we may need help finding that answer, but it is within us. These are golden nuggets of truth.

Did you know?

That the words we speak do bring forth life or death and that the POWER OF LIFE in the spirit is the tongue.

Did you know?

Lack of communication and building loving relationships is the number one problem in resolving discord and spiritual problems.

These are facts, search them out.

Anita

My Blessing to My Readers

"The Lord bless you and keep you:
The Lord make His face to shine upon you,
And be gracious to you,
The Lord lift up his countenance upon you,
And give you peace." Numbers 6:24-26
Receive — Selah, Anita

About the Author

Anita F. Mason

Anita F. Mason MA, LMFT, D. Min, is a Licensed Marital and Family Therapist. Anita is a graduate of the University of Illinois where she earned a B.A. in Psychology and an M.A. in Family Therapy. She counsels in therapeutic Intervention of all types, and also specialized training in trauma and crisis.

Anita earned a Doctorate in Practical Ministry through Wagner Leadership Institute. She also received a Certificate of Licensing from Barbara Wentroble, Dr. Chuck Pierce and Robert Heidler of Glory of Zion Outreach Ministries, Inc.

Anita is Founder and President of Joshua Company, Women Mentoring Women, First Friday Praise and Worship, Sons of Joshua (men's group), and My Father's House Healing Room.

For more information, go to: www.joshuacompanyministries.com Or contact us at joshuacompany@aol.com or (217) 422-3524.

CPSIA information can be obtained at www.ICGtesting.com
Printed in the USA
BVOW071534160513

320915BV00001B/1/P